RAMADHAAN LESSONS

FROM THE NOBLE QURAN AND AUTHENTIC SUNNAH

VOLUME TWO: 1440 (2019)

PREPARED BY: MOOSAA RICHARDSON

First Print Edition: Sha'baan 1440 (April 2019)

Richardson, Moosaa.

Ramadhaan Lessons From the Noble Quran and Authentic Sunnah, Vol.2 / Author: Moosaa Richardson.

ISBN: 978-1094801278

1. Nonfiction —Religion —Islam —Koran & Sacred Writings.

2. Education & Reference —Study Aids —General.

TABLE OF CONTENTS

INTRODUCTION   5

LESSON 1: From the Traits of the Hypocrites   7

LESSON 2: The Man with Two Faces   11

LESSON 3: The Changing of the *Qiblah* Direction   15

LESSON 4: Prayer to the Wrong Direction by Mistake   19

LESSON 5: A Treasure from Beneath the Throne   21

LESSON 6: Making Distinctions Between Prophets   25

LESSON 7: Hastening to Allah's Forgiveness   29

LESSON 8: Being Patient With People's Harms   33

LESSON 9: The Importance of *Hijrah* (Emigration)   37

LESSON 10: Is There Any Repentance for Mass Murderers?   41

LESSON 11: Islamic Punishments for Terrorists   45

LESSON 12: The Story of the Criminals from 'Uraynah   49

LESSON 13: Only Allah Has All Knowledge of the Unseen   53

LESSON 14: He Came to Teach the People Their Religion   57

LESSON 15: Ten Commandments in the Quran   59

LESSON 16: Following Allah's Straight Path   63

LESSON 17: True Believers Described in Detail   65

LESSON 18: The Seven Shaded Under Allah's Throne   69

LESSON 19: How Religious Allies Must Interact   73

LESSON 20: Focusing on Yourself Primarily, Not Exclusively   77

LESSON 21: Allah Alone Controls All Benefit and Harm   81

LESSON 22: Obedience to Allah & True Reliance Upon Him   85

LESSON 23: A Reminder for All Those Who Remember   89

LESSON 24: Piety, Repentance, and Good Manners   93

LESSON 25: The Great Merits of Upright Speech   97

LESSON 26: The Seeds From Which the Trees of Paradise Grow   103

LESSON 27: The Futility of False Objects of Worship   105

LESSON 28: Closing Off the Pathways to Polytheism   109

LESSON 29: Islam Emphasizes Individual Accountability   113

LESSON 30: Supplicating for Ten Important Things   117

A FINAL WORD   121

INDEX OF SHAYKH IBN BAAZ'S FATWAS   128

INTRODUCTION

All praise is due to Allah, the Lord, Creator, and Sustainer of all things. May He raise the rank of and grant peace to the final seal of all of His Prophets and Messengers, Muhammad, and all of his respected family and noble companions.

As we approach Ramadhaan, the month of fasting, the month of the Quran, the month of *taqwa* (piety), the month of Divine Forgiveness and nearness to Allah, we beg our Gracious and Merciful Lord that He bestow upon us sincerity, understanding of His Magnificent Book, the Quran, and actions and statements that He loves and is pleased with.

We praise Allah and thank Him for the tremendous level of success we enjoyed with last year's Ramadhaan lessons. They were held locally at al-Masjid al-Awwal in Pittsburgh, Pennsylvania and broadcast live internationally. Thousands of workbooks, in print and on Kindle, were distributed all over the world. Thousands of people attended the daily live broadcasts or downloaded the lessons. We ask Allah to accept from us and all of them!

We listened carefully to feedback and planned this year's lessons to build on the best of last year.

While many students truly enjoyed the Arabic Language modules with each lesson last year, a considerable number of people struggled to get benefit from them. So Arabic enthusiasts: We have bad news and good news for you! The bad news is that we have removed the Arabic modules from within this year's Ramadhaan lessons. However, the good news is that we are preparing a new resource, a complete study course of the classic *Aajurroomiyyah* Primer, with workbook and recordings, slated for publication in 1441, *in shaa' Allah*.

This year's Ramadhaan Lessons, like last year's, are another mix of various topics of importance: Creed, Methodology, *Fiqh*, Manners, etc., presented as either *Tafseer* of Quranic passages or explanations of Hadeeth narrations. A heavy focus is given to reminders and admonitions throughout; the influence of and reliance upon the works of Shaykh Muhammad ibn Saalih al-'Uthaymeen (may Allah have Mercy on him) should be apparent. Additionally, this year's lessons include an interesting new feature: A daily *fatwa* (edict) from the *Fatwa* Collection of Shaykh 'Abdul-'Azeez ibn Baaz (may Allah have Mercy on him). An index of the *fatwa* topics has been provided on page 128.

It is important to note that this workbook was not designed for independent self-study. To maximize your benefit from these lessons, attend in person, or download or listen to the recordings of the live 1440 Ramadhaan Lessons, and follow along using this workbook. Here is how you can benefit from the live broadcasts and/or their recordings:

Go to **www.Spreaker.com/radio1mm** and click on the **"SHOWS"** menu, as illustrated below:

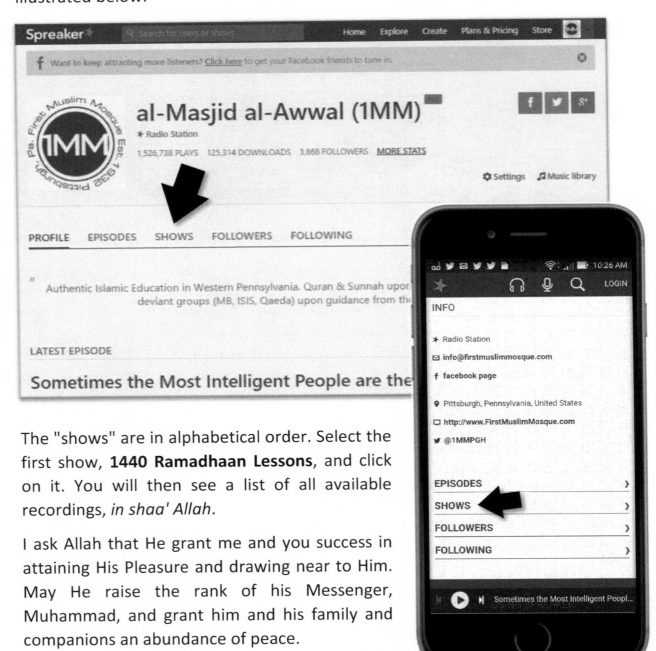

The "shows" are in alphabetical order. Select the first show, **1440 Ramadhaan Lessons**, and click on it. You will then see a list of all available recordings, *in shaa' Allah*.

I ask Allah that He grant me and you success in attaining His Pleasure and drawing near to Him. May He raise the rank of his Messenger, Muhammad, and grant him and his family and companions an abundance of peace.

ABUL-'ABBAAS MOOSAA RICHARDSON

Education Director of the First Muslim Mosque of Pittsburgh, Pennsylvania

1.1 QURANIC PASSAGE & TRANSLATION

وَإِذَا قِيلَ لَهُمْ ءَامِنُوا كَمَآ ءَامَنَ ٱلنَّاسُ قَالُوٓا أَنُؤْمِنُ كَمَآ ءَامَنَ ٱلسُّفَهَآءُ أَلَآ إِنَّهُمْ هُمُ ٱلسُّفَهَآءُ وَلَـٰكِن لَّا يَعْلَمُونَ ﴿١٣﴾ وَإِذَا لَقُوا ٱلَّذِينَ ءَامَنُوا قَالُوٓا ءَامَنَّا وَإِذَا خَلَوْا إِلَىٰ شَيَـٰطِينِهِمْ قَالُوٓا إِنَّا مَعَكُمْ إِنَّمَا نَحْنُ مُسْتَهْزِءُونَ ﴿١٤﴾ ٱللَّهُ يَسْتَهْزِئُ بِهِمْ وَيَمُدُّهُمْ فِى طُغْيَـٰنِهِمْ يَعْمَهُونَ ﴿١٥﴾ أُوْلَـٰٓئِكَ ٱلَّذِينَ ٱشْتَرَوُا ٱلضَّلَـٰلَةَ بِٱلْهُدَىٰ فَمَا رَبِحَت تِّجَـٰرَتُهُمْ وَمَا كَانُوا مُهْتَدِينَ ﴿١٦﴾ (البقرة)

When it is said to them, "Believe as the people have believed," They say, "Should we believe as fools do!?" Nay, it is they who are actually the fools, yet they do not even know. When they meet up with the people who believe, they say, "We [also] believe." Yet when they go off in secret to their devils, they say, "We are really with you; we were only mocking [the believers]." Allah ridicules them and increases their misguided transgressions in which they stumble about aimlessly. Such are those who have purchased misguidance with the guidance [they had], and so their trade earned no profit, nor were they rightly guided. (2:13-16)

1.2 TAFSEER BENEFITS

1) When it is said to "them"
2) Definition of hypocrisy
3) Why we learn the attributes of hypocrites

4) The invitation to *eemaan* is for everyone.	
5) Who are "the people"?	
6) Traits of hypocrisy from this passage 1 2 3 4 5 6	7 8 9 10 11 12 13
7) "Nay, it is they who are actually the fools"	
8) Name-calling used to run people away	
9) Allah defends the believers	
10) Extended meaning of "fool"	
11) Being wise & rightly guided	
12) Mockery as a divine Attribute	
13) Respite given to transgressors	
14) "Those are the ones..."	
15) The greatest loss ever (18:103-106)	

1.3 RESEARCH: Review Lesson 19 from last year's *RAMADHAAN LESSSONS* (Vol.1, 1439). Then, summarize the attributes of hypocrites which are exposed in *Soorah al-Munaafiqoon* (and elsewhere) in the table below.

63:1	They testify openly, but Allah knows their inner reality.
63:1	They are liars.
63:2	They hide behind their oaths.
63:2	They obstruct people from the path of Allah.
63:3	

1.4 FATWA: Shaykh 'Abdul-'Azeez ibn Baaz (may Allah have Mercy on him) was asked the following question. Listen and summarize his answer in the box below.

Question: How many witnesses are required to establish the sighting of the crescent moon of Ramadhaan?

Shaykh Ibn Baaz replied:

2.1 HADEETH & TRANSLATION

عَنْ أَبِي هُرَيْرَةَ رَضِيَ اللهُ عَنْهُ، عَنِ النَّبِيِّ صَلَّى اللهُ عَلَيْهِ وَسَلَّمَ، قَالَ: «تَجِدُونَ النَّاسَ مَعَادِنَ: فَخِيَارُهُمْ فِي الْجَاهِلِيَّةِ خِيَارُهُمْ فِي الْإِسْلَامِ إِذَا فَقِهُوا؛ وَتَجِدُونَ مِنْ خَيْرِ النَّاسِ فِي هَذَا الْأَمْرِ، أَكْرَهُهُمْ لَهُ، قَبْلَ أَنْ يَقَعَ فِيهِ، وَتَجِدُونَ مِنْ شِرَارِ النَّاسِ ذَا الْوَجْهَيْنِ، الَّذِي يَأْتِي هؤُلَاءِ بِوَجْهٍ وَهؤُلَاءِ بِوَجْهٍ.» (مُتَّفَقٌ عَلَيْهِ)

On the authority of Aboo Hurayrah (may Allah be pleased with him): The Prophet (may Allah raise his rank and grant him peace) said: **"You will find the people to be different types: The best of them in *Jaahiliyyah* (the pre-Islamic era of ignorance) are the best of them in Islam, so long as they have gained understanding** [of Islamic rulings and principles]. **You will find that from the best of the people in this affair are those who hated it the most, before they entered into it. And you will find that among the worst of the people is the two-faced person; he comes to these people with one face, and to those people with a different face."** (Agreed upon)

2.2 BENEFITS OF THE HADEETH

1) Aboo Hurayrah
2) Agreed upon
3) Like different rocks/minerals (literally)
4) Muslims are on different levels of knowledge and religiosity. (Hadeeth)

5) The importance of gaining *Fiqh* (understanding)

   (Hadeeth)

6) "Those who hate it the most"

   (Hadeeth)

   (Athar)

7) Two-facedness detailed in Quran 2:14

8) A specific punishment in the Hereafter for two-facedness

   (Hadeeth)

9) Playing both sides of the fence

10) The extent of the evil sown by such a person

11) He is more evil than either party he pretends to be with

12) The legal testimony of a two-faced person

   (2:282)

   (Hadeeth)

13) Understanding what some people consider a clash

   (Hadeeth)

14) How to improve our character, in light of this discussion

2.3 LEARN AN AUTHENTIC SUPPLICATION: The following supplication was collected by al-Haakim, al-Bayhaqee, and others. It was classified as authentic by al-Albaanee in *Saheeh al-Jaami' as-Sagheer* (no.1285).

O Allah! I seek refuge with You from incapability, laziness, cowardice, stinginess, senility, harshness, heedlessness, poverty, humiliation, and abjection.

اللّهُمَّ إِنِّي أَعُوذُ بِكَ مِنَ الْعَجْزِ وَالْكَسَلِ، وَالْجُبْنِ وَالْبُخْلِ، وَالْهَرَمِ وَالْقَسْوَةِ، وَالْغَفْلَةِ وَالْعَيْلَةِ، وَالذِّلَّةِ وَالْمَسْكَنَةِ؛

I also seek refuge with You from destitution [of the soul], disbelief, disobedience, division, hypocrisy, and desiring to be heard or seen.

وَأَعُوذُ بِكَ مِنَ الْفَقْرِ وَالْكُفْرِ، وَالْفُسُوقِ، وَالشِّقَاقِ، وَالنِّفَاقِ، وَالسُّمْعَةِ، وَالرِّيَاءِ؛

And I seek refuge with you from deafness, being mute, insanity, leprosy, skin disease, and the worst of illnesses.

وَأَعُوذُ بِكَ مِنَ الصَّمَمِ وَالْبَكَمِ، وَالْجُنُونِ، وَالْجُذَامِ، وَالْبَرَصِ، وَسَيِّئِ الْأَسْقَامِ.

2.4 FATWA: Shaykh 'Abdul-'Azeez ibn Baaz (may Allah have Mercy on him) was asked the following question. Listen and summarize his answer in the box below.

Question: Is it permissible to ignore the moon sightings and rely solely upon scientific calculations to plan the beginning of Ramadhaan?

Shaykh Ibn Baaz replied:

The First Muslim Mosque (Al-Masjid Al-Awwal), est. 1932, located in the heart of Pittsburgh's historic Hill District, hosts a vibrant community of local and international congregants, adhering to the tenants of Orthodox Islam, actively condemning terrorist organizations such as ISIS, Alqaeda, and the (so-called) Muslim Brotherhood.

TWITTER: @1MMPGH

WEBSITE: WWW.FIRSTMUSLIMMOSQUE.COM

EMAIL: INFO@FIRSTMUSLIMMOSQUE.COM

3.1 QURANIC PASSAGE & TRANSLATION

سَيَقُولُ ٱلسُّفَهَآءُ مِنَ ٱلنَّاسِ مَا وَلَّىٰهُمْ عَن قِبْلَتِهِمُ ٱلَّتِى كَانُوا۟ عَلَيْهَا قُل لِّلَّهِ ٱلْمَشْرِقُ وَٱلْمَغْرِبُ يَهْدِى مَن يَشَآءُ إِلَىٰ صِرَٰطٍ مُّسْتَقِيمٍ ۝ وَكَذَٰلِكَ جَعَلْنَٰكُمْ أُمَّةً وَسَطًا لِّتَكُونُوا۟ شُهَدَآءَ عَلَى ٱلنَّاسِ وَيَكُونَ ٱلرَّسُولُ عَلَيْكُمْ شَهِيدًا وَمَا جَعَلْنَا ٱلْقِبْلَةَ ٱلَّتِى كُنتَ عَلَيْهَآ إِلَّا لِنَعْلَمَ مَن يَتَّبِعُ ٱلرَّسُولَ مِمَّن يَنقَلِبُ عَلَىٰ عَقِبَيْهِ وَإِن كَانَتْ لَكَبِيرَةً إِلَّا عَلَى ٱلَّذِينَ هَدَى ٱللَّهُ وَمَا كَانَ ٱللَّهُ لِيُضِيعَ إِيمَٰنَكُمْ إِنَّ ٱللَّهَ بِٱلنَّاسِ لَرَءُوفٌ رَّحِيمٌ ۝ (البقرة)

The fools among men will say: "What has turned them away from their *qiblah* (direction), the one they used to face?" Say: "To Allah belongs the East and the West. He guides whomsoever He wills to a straight path." As such We have made you a balanced nation, to be witnesses over the people, and so the Messenger would be, over you all, a witness. And We have not made the previous *qiblah* you faced except as a matter through which We make known those who follow the Messenger from those who turn on their heels. It was indeed a huge matter [of difficulty], except upon those whom Allah has guided. And Allah would not allow your faith to be lost. Verily, Allah is indeed Ever Compassionate, Ever Merciful. (2:142-143)

3.2 TAFSEER BENEFITS

1) Who are the "fools among men"?
2) Allah foretells their statement before they utter it.
3) The previous *qiblah*
4) "To Allah belongs the East and the West"

5) "A straight path"
6) Preparing someone for what is coming
7) Explaining some matters by *Ruboobiyyah* alone

8) Guidance is of two basic types:
 	
   (28:56)
 	
   (42:52)

9) The virtue of those guided back to the original *qiblah*   (3:96)

10) The meaning of this Ummah being balanced
 	
   In creed:
 	
   In *Fiqh*:

11) Muslims as witnesses over Mankind
12) The Prophet (صلى الله عليه وسلم) as a witness over us
13) The definite article in the wording: "THE Messenger"
14) "We make known those who..."
15) The meaning of following
16) "From those who turn on their heels"
17) The meaning of "your faith"

18) The Creed of *Ahlus-Sunnah* about *Eemaan*
19) Two Names and their Attributes A) B)
20) Being tested through Allah's Rulings A) B) C)
21) The general obligation of following: (33:36) (4:65) (24:51)
22) Faith makes difficult tasks easy
23) Our actions are preserved and not lost
24) An example of abrogation (*naskh*)

3.3 FATWA: Shaykh 'Abdul-'Azeez ibn Baaz (may Allah have Mercy on him) was asked the following question. Listen and summarize his answer in the box below.

Question: What if someone starting fasting in a land that began fasting with a moon sighting, and then traveled to another land where they began fasting after a full 30 days of Sha'baan, and then he ends up fasting 31 days because of this?

Shaykh Ibn Baaz replied:

4.1 HADEETH & TRANSLATION

عَنْ عَامِرِ بْنِ رَبِيعَةَ ــ رَضِيَ اللهُ عَنْهُ ــ ، قَالَ: كُنَّا مَعَ النَّبِيّ ــ صَلَّى اللهُ عَلَيْهِ وَسَلَّمَ ــ فِي سَفَرٍ فِي لَيْلَةٍ مُظْلِمَةٍ، فَلَمْ نَدْرِ أَيْنَ الْقِبْلَةُ، فَصَلَّى كُلُّ رَجُلٍ مِنَّا عَلَى حِيَالِهِ، فَلَمَّا أَصْبَحْنَا ذَكَرْنَا ذَلِكَ لِلنَّبِيّ ــ صَلَّى اللهُ عَلَيْهِ وَسَلَّمَ ــ ، فَنَزَلَ: {فَأَيْنَمَا تُوَلُّوا فَثَمَّ وَجْهُ اللهِ} (البقرة: ١١٥). (أَخْرَجَهُ التِّرْمِذِيُّ، وَضَعَّفَ إِسْنَادَهُ، وَحَسَّنَهُ الْأَلْبَانِيُّ بِطُرُقِهِ.).

On the authority of 'Aamir ibn Rabee'ah (may Allah be pleased with him), who said: We were with the Prophet (may Allah raise his rank and grant him peace) during a journey on a very dark night, and we could not determine the qiblah. So each one of us prayed in a different direction. In the morning, we mentioned that to the Prophet (may Allah raise his rank and grant him peace), and so it was revealed: **"Whichever direction you turn, there is the Face of Allah."** (2:115) (At-Tirmithee)

4.2 BENEFITS OF THE HADEETH

1) 'Aamir ibn Rabee'ah
2) At-Tirmithee
3) Authenticity of the hadeeth At-Tirmithee's original verdict on this chain: Al-Albaanee's research:

4) The positions of the scholars on this hadeeth.
5) The ease of Islamic rulings

4.3 FATWA: Shaykh 'Abdul-'Azeez ibn Baaz (may Allah have Mercy on him) was asked the following question. Listen and summarize his answer in the box below.

Question: Is the fasting possibly valid from a person who does not offer the five daily prayers?

> **Shaykh Ibn Baaz replied:**

5.1 QURANIC PASSAGE & TRANSLATION

ءَامَنَ ٱلرَّسُولُ بِمَآ أُنزِلَ إِلَيْهِ مِن رَّبِّهِۦ وَٱلْمُؤْمِنُونَ ۚ كُلٌّ ءَامَنَ بِٱللَّهِ وَمَلَـٰٓئِكَتِهِۦ وَكُتُبِهِۦ وَرُسُلِهِۦ لَا نُفَرِّقُ بَيْنَ أَحَدٍ مِّن رُّسُلِهِۦ ۚ وَقَالُوا۟ سَمِعْنَا وَأَطَعْنَا ۖ غُفْرَانَكَ رَبَّنَا وَإِلَيْكَ ٱلْمَصِيرُ ۝ لَا يُكَلِّفُ ٱللَّهُ نَفْسًا إِلَّا وُسْعَهَا ۚ لَهَا مَا كَسَبَتْ وَعَلَيْهَا مَا ٱكْتَسَبَتْ ۗ رَبَّنَا لَا تُؤَاخِذْنَآ إِن نَّسِينَآ أَوْ أَخْطَأْنَا ۚ رَبَّنَا وَلَا تَحْمِلْ عَلَيْنَآ إِصْرًا كَمَا حَمَلْتَهُۥ عَلَى ٱلَّذِينَ مِن قَبْلِنَا ۚ رَبَّنَا وَلَا تُحَمِّلْنَا مَا لَا طَاقَةَ لَنَا بِهِۦ ۖ وَٱعْفُ عَنَّا وَٱغْفِرْ لَنَا وَٱرْحَمْنَآ ۚ أَنتَ مَوْلَىٰنَا فَٱنصُرْنَا عَلَى ٱلْقَوْمِ ٱلْكَـٰفِرِينَ ۝ (البقرة)

The Messenger believes in what was revealed to him from His Lord, as do the believers. All of them believe in Allah, His Angels, His Books, and His Messengers. "We make no distinction between any of the Messengers," And they say, "We hear and obey. We ask for Your Forgiveness, our Lord! And unto You Alone is the return." Allah does not burden any soul except with what it is capable of. It shall have what it earns [of reward], and it shall bear whatever burden [of sin] it deserves. "Our Lord, do not hold us accountable if we forget or err. Our Lord, do not place a burden upon us as You placed burdens on those before us. Our Lord, do not burden us with what we have no ability to fulfill, and excuse us, forgive us, and have Mercy on us. You Alone are our Protector, so give us victory over the disbelieving people." (2:285-286)

5.2 TAFSEER BENEFITS

1) The meaning of belief (*eemaan*)
2) "THE Messenger..."

3) What was revealed to him (4:113)	A) B)
4) "From his Lord" (*Ruboobiyyah*) General: (1:1)	Exclusive: (25:63)
5) The believers believe in three things: A)	B) C)
6) The believers are praised in four ways: A) B)	C) D)
7) Belief in Allah is four basic matters: A) B)	C) D)
8) Belief in the Angels (66:6)	
9) Belief in the books A) The _____ sent to _____ B) The _____ sent to _____	C) The _____ sent to _____ D) The _____ sent to _____ E) The _____ sent to _____
10) The number of Prophets and Messengers (Hadeeth)	
11) An interesting linguistic tool: *"iltifaat"*	
12) Not making distinctions between the Messengers	

13) "We hear and obey..."   (24:51)

14) "We ask for Your Forgiveness..."
 	
   The meaning of "*maghfirah*"
 	
   (47:19)
 	
   (Hadeeth)

15) "Unto You Alone is the Return"
16) Rewards earned and punishment deserved   (Hadeeth)
17) Allah's Response to the supplication   (Hadeeth)

18) No accountability for errors or forgetfulness
 	
   (Hadeeth)
 	
   (Hadeeth)
 	
   (Hadeeth)

19) Two Names and their Attributes
 	
   A)
 	
   B)

20) Victory over disbelievers
21) Confirmation of Allah's Loftiness
22) Focus on Lordship and servitude throughout
23) What about the two other pillars of faith not mentioned? (_____ & _____)   Reply #1:

Reply #2:
24) The foundation for an Usool principle
25) Individual responsibility for one's actions (53:36-39)
26) Three necessary requests: A) B) C)
27) Specific virtues of these two Verses: A) B) C) D)

5.3 FATWA: Shaykh 'Abdul-'Azeez ibn Baaz (may Allah have Mercy on him) was asked the following question. Listen and summarize his answer in the box below.

Question: Should we instruct our young children to fast?

Shaykh Ibn Baaz replied:

6.1 HADEETH & TRANSLATION

عَنْ أَبِي سَعِيدٍ الْخُدْرِيِّ ـ رَضِيَ اللهُ عَنْهُ ـ ، قَالَ: بَيْنَمَا رَسُولُ اللهِ ـ صَلَّى اللهُ عَلَيْهِ وَسَلَّمَ ـ جَالِسٌ جَاءَ رَجُلٌ يَهُودِيٌّ، فَقَالَ: يَا أَبَا الْقَاسِمِ! ضَرَبَ وَجْهِي رَجُلٌ مِنْ أَصْحَابِكَ! فَقَالَ: «مَنْ؟» قَالَ: رَجُلٌ مِنَ الْأَنْصَارِ. قَالَ: «ادْعُوهُ.» فَقَالَ: «أَضَرَبْتَهُ؟» قَالَ: سَمِعْتُهُ بِالسُّوقِ يَحْلِفُ: وَالَّذِي اصْطَفَى مُوسَى عَلَى الْبَشَرِ، قُلْتُ: أَيْ خَبِيثُ! عَلَى مُحَمَّدٍ ـ صَلَّى اللهُ عَلَيْهِ وَسَلَّمَ ـ !؟ فَأَخَذَتْنِي غَضْبَةٌ، ضَرَبْتُ وَجْهَهُ. فَقَالَ النَّبِيُّ ـ صَلَّى اللهُ عَلَيْهِ وَسَلَّمَ ـ : «لَا تُخَيِّرُوا بَيْنَ الْأَنْبِيَاءِ، فَإِنَّ النَّاسَ يَصْعَقُونَ يَوْمَ الْقِيَامَةِ، فَأَكُونُ أَوَّلَ مَنْ تَنْشَقُّ عَنْهُ الْأَرْضُ، فَإِذَا أَنَا بِمُوسَى آخِذٌ بِقَائِمَةٍ مِنْ قَوَائِمِ الْعَرْشِ، فَلَا أَدْرِي أَكَانَ فِيمَنْ صَعِقَ، أَمْ حُوسِبَ بِصَعْقَةِ الْأُولَى؟» (مُتَّفَقٌ عَلَيْهِ، وَهَذَا لَفْظُ الْبُخَارِيِّ.)

On the authority of Aboo Sa'eed al-Khudree (may Allah be pleased with him), who said: When the Prophet (may Allah raise his rank and grant him peace) was sitting once, a Jew came and said: "O Abal-Qaasim! One of your companions struck me in the face!" He asked, **"Who?"** He replied, "One of the Ansaar." He said, **"Call him here."** He then asked him, **"Did you strike him?"** He replied, "I heard him in the marketplace swearing by the One who favored Moosaa over all of humanity, so I said: You filthy man! Over Muhammad (may Allah raise his rank and grant him peace)?! I was overtaken by a moment of anger, and so I struck his face." So the Prophet (may Allah raise his rank and grant him peace) said: **"Do not make distinctions between the prophets, because the people will have all collapsed on the Day of Judgment, and I will be the first one to rise from the grave. I will find myself there with Moosaa, holding onto the legs of the Throne, and I will not know if he had been from those who collapsed, or if the first collapse sufficed him."** (Agreed upon)

6.2 BENEFITS OF THE HADEETH

1) Aboo Sa'eed al-Khudree
2) "Agreed upon"
3) Allah has made distinctions between Prophets: (2:253) (17:55)
4) He forbade us from making distinctions between them. (2:136)
5) We affirm the distinctions Allah gave them. (Hadeeth)
6) A distinction in following (5:48)
7) The lofty status of Prophet Moosaa (33:69)
8) Moosaa was "exempted"?
9) "Or the first collapse sufficed him"?
10) Jews coming for legal verdicts
11) A judge hears both sides of the story
12) Verdicts not based on religious brotherhood
13) Mentioning virtues to defend someone's honor

6.3 RESEARCH: Compile the names of the Prophets as found in the Quran.

1	2:31	ADAM	"And He (Allah) taught **ADAM** the names of all things..."
2			

6.4 FATWA: Shaykh 'Abdul-'Azeez ibn Baaz (may Allah have Mercy on him) was asked the following question. Listen and summarize his answer in the box below.

Question: What does a women do when she delayed making her days of Ramadhaan up until the next Ramadhaan came?

Shaykh Ibn Baaz replied:

7.1 QURANIC PASSAGE & TRANSLATION

﴿ ۞ وَسَارِعُوٓاْ إِلَىٰ مَغْفِرَةٍ مِّن رَّبِّكُمْ وَجَنَّةٍ عَرْضُهَا ٱلسَّمَٰوَٰتُ وَٱلْأَرْضُ أُعِدَّتْ لِلْمُتَّقِينَ ۝ ٱلَّذِينَ يُنفِقُونَ فِى ٱلسَّرَّآءِ وَٱلضَّرَّآءِ وَٱلْكَٰظِمِينَ ٱلْغَيْظَ وَٱلْعَافِينَ عَنِ ٱلنَّاسِ ۗ وَٱللَّهُ يُحِبُّ ٱلْمُحْسِنِينَ ۝ وَٱلَّذِينَ إِذَا فَعَلُواْ فَٰحِشَةً أَوْ ظَلَمُوٓاْ أَنفُسَهُمْ ذَكَرُواْ ٱللَّهَ فَٱسْتَغْفَرُواْ لِذُنُوبِهِمْ وَمَن يَغْفِرُ ٱلذُّنُوبَ إِلَّا ٱللَّهُ وَلَمْ يُصِرُّواْ عَلَىٰ مَا فَعَلُواْ وَهُمْ يَعْلَمُونَ ۝ أُوْلَٰٓئِكَ جَزَآؤُهُم مَّغْفِرَةٌ مِّن رَّبِّهِمْ وَجَنَّٰتٌ تَجْرِى مِن تَحْتِهَا ٱلْأَنْهَٰرُ خَٰلِدِينَ فِيهَا ۚ وَنِعْمَ أَجْرُ ٱلْعَٰمِلِينَ ۝ ﴾ (آل عمران)

Race one another towards Forgiveness from your Lord and a garden as wide as the heavens and the earth, prepared for the pious, those who spend in times of both ease and hardship, those who restrain their anger, and those who excuse people. Allah loves those who are kind. And when they commit an obscenity or oppress themselves, they remember Allah and seek forgiveness for their sins. And who forgives sins other than Allah? And they do not persist in what they have done, when they know [better]. Such people shall have their reward of Forgiveness from their Lord and gardens under which rivers flow, abiding therein forever. What a fine reward for those who work [diligently]! (3:133-136)

7.2 TAFSEER BENEFITS

1) A similar Quranic passage   (57:21)
2) Hastening towards Allah's Forgiveness

3) This obligation is effective immediately.

(2:248)

The Usool principle about orders:

---

4) Those who hasten forth towards good

(21:90)

(23:61)

---

5) Those who hasten forth into evil

(5:41)

(4:83)

(49:6)

(Hadeeth)

---

6) Paradise has already been created.

---

7) The people of *taqwa* and their reward

---

8) Attributes of the people of *taqwa*:

1.

2.

3.

4.

5.

6.

7.

---

9) "Those who spend in both times of ease and hardship..."

A) In time of ease:

B) In times of hardship:

---

10) Restraining one's anger is true inner strength.

(Hadeeth)

---

11) Excusing others hoping to be excused

(42:40)

12) *Ihsaan* is accomplished in two basic ways:
 	
  A) In worship
 	
  B) In interactions with people

13) Remembering Allah after a lapse in piety
14) Asking Allah for Forgiveness   (4:110)
15) People of *taqwa* are not perfect.   (Hadeeth)

16) The three conditions of repentance in these Verses:
 	
  A)
 	
  B)
 	
  C)

17) "Gardens under which rivers flow"
18) "Abiding therein forever"
19) "What a fine reward for those who work"   A refutation of the *Murji'ah* Cult

7.3 FATWA: Shaykh 'Abdul-'Azeez ibn Baaz (may Allah have Mercy on him) was asked the following question. Listen and summarize his answer in the box below.

Question: I reached puberty when I was 12, but my family never instructed me to start fasting until I was 14? What do I do?

Shaykh Ibn Baaz replied:

8.1 HADEETH & TRANSLATION

عَنِ ابْنِ عُمَرَ ـ رَضِيَ اللهُ عَنْهُمَا ـ قَالَ: قَالَ رَسُولُ اللهِ ـ صَلَّى اللهُ عَلَيْهِ وَسَلَّمَ ـ :

«المُؤْمِنُ الَّذِي يُخَالِطُ النَّاسَ وَيَصْبِرُ عَلَى أَذَاهُمْ أَعْظَمُ أَجْرًا مِنَ الَّذِي لَا يُخَالِطُ

النَّاسَ وَلَا يَصْبِرُ عَلَى أَذَاهُمْ.» (أَخْرَجَهُ أَحْمَدُ وَالتِّرْمِذِيُّ وَابْنُ مَاجَهْ، وَصَحَّحَهُ الأَلْبَانِيُّ)

On the authority of Ibn 'Umar (may Allah be pleased with him and his father), who said: The Prophet (may Allah raise his rank and grant him peace) said: **"The believer who mixes with the people and bears their harms patiently is greater in reward than the one who does not mix with the people nor bear their harms patiently."** (Ahmad, at-Tirmithee, Ibn Maajah)

8.2 BENEFITS OF THE HADEETH

1) Ibn 'Umar
2) *Imams* of hadeeth who collected it: B) at-Tirmithee A) Ahmad C) Ibn Maajah
3) Authenticity
4) Believers categorized into two groups: A) B)
5) At times, staying away from people may be better: (73:10) (4:140) (6:68)

(Hadeeth)

How to know what is best:

---

6) Allah orders us to be patient with people's harms.

(18:28)

(31:17)

---

7) The status of patient people with Allah

(2:153)

(3:146)

---

8) Paradise is for the patient people

(13:22-24)

---

9) "Greater in reward" – How much greater?

(39:10)

---

10) Ramadhan & patience: Connect a hadeeth about the unlimited reward of fasting to the previous Verse.

---

11) A neglected Sunnah of the Companions

8.3 RESEARCH: Summarize Shaykh al-Islam Ibn Taymiyah's "20 Keys to Patience with the Harms of the People" in the table below.

1	Affirming towheed & submitting to Allah's Qadr in all matters
2	Remembering and critically revisiting one's own sinful behavior
3	
4	
5	
6	
7	
8	
9	
10	
11	
12	
13	
14	
15	
16	
17	
18	
19	
20	

8.4 FATWA: Shaykh 'Abdul-'Azeez ibn Baaz (may Allah have Mercy on him) was asked the following question. Listen and summarize his answer in the box below.

Question: Can a woman fast if her menses just ended before Fajr?

Shaykh Ibn Baaz replied:

9.1 QURANIC PASSAGE & TRANSLATION

إِنَّ الَّذِينَ تَوَفَّاهُمُ الْمَلَائِكَةُ ظَالِمِي أَنفُسِهِمْ قَالُوا فِيمَ كُنتُمْ قَالُوا كُنَّا مُسْتَضْعَفِينَ فِي الْأَرْضِ قَالُوا أَلَمْ تَكُنْ أَرْضُ اللَّهِ وَاسِعَةً فَتُهَاجِرُوا فِيهَا فَأُولَٰئِكَ مَأْوَاهُمْ جَهَنَّمُ وَسَاءَتْ مَصِيرًا ۝ إِلَّا الْمُسْتَضْعَفِينَ مِنَ الرِّجَالِ وَالنِّسَاءِ وَالْوِلْدَانِ لَا يَسْتَطِيعُونَ حِيلَةً وَلَا يَهْتَدُونَ سَبِيلًا ۝ فَأُولَٰئِكَ عَسَى اللَّهُ أَن يَعْفُوَ عَنْهُمْ وَكَانَ اللَّهُ عَفُوًّا غَفُورًا ۝ وَمَن يُهَاجِرْ فِي سَبِيلِ اللَّهِ يَجِدْ فِي الْأَرْضِ مُرَاغَمًا كَثِيرًا وَسَعَةً وَمَن يَخْرُجْ مِن بَيْتِهِ مُهَاجِرًا إِلَى اللَّهِ وَرَسُولِهِ ثُمَّ يُدْرِكْهُ الْمَوْتُ فَقَدْ وَقَعَ أَجْرُهُ عَلَى اللَّهِ وَكَانَ اللَّهُ غَفُورًا رَّحِيمًا ۝ (النساء)

Verily, those whose souls are taken by the Angels, self-oppressive, they say to them: "What were you doing?" They claim, "We were oppressed in the land." They say, "Was not Allah's earth spacious enough for you to emigrate elsewhere?" The abode of such people is *Jahannam*, what an evil destination! Exempted are the truly oppressed among men, women, and children who could not find the strength to emigrate nor locate its path. Such people will be excused by Allah, and Allah is Ever Excusing, All-Forgiving. And whoever does emigrate in the Way of Allah will find in the land many fine places to dwell and abundant provisions. Whoever leaves his house as an emigrant to Allah and His Messenger, yet death overtakes him, then verily his reward lies with Allah. And Allah is All-Forgiving, Ever Merciful. (4:97-100)

9.2 TAFSEER BENEFITS

1) The incident about which the Verses were revealed

2) The Angel of Death and his assistants

   (32:11)

   (8:50)

3) Regarding the Arabic word: تَوَفَّهُمُ

4) The three kinds of people:

   (35:32)

5) "What were you doing?"

6) Their claim of being oppressed and weak

7) Some excuses are legitimate, others are not.

8) The divine encouragement to emigrate

   (29:56)

9) Is *hijrah* an obligation even today?

10) A principle regarding divine threats of punishment

11) A confirmation of our belief in the Angels

12) Those legitimately excused

   (Hadeeth)

13) Those who "could not find the strength to emigrate..."

14) "Nor locate its path"
15) Regarding the Arabic phrase: عَسَى ٱللَّهُ أَن يَعۡفُوَ عَنۡهُمۡ
16) No sin in the absence of capability (64:16) (Hadeeth)
17) An intention stipulated (Hadeeth)
18) Worldly ease and provisions promised
19) Repeating the topic of *hijrah* and its intention (Hadeeth)
20) "His reward lies with Allah" (Hadeeth)
21) Two Divine Names at the end of the Verse A) B)

9.3 FATWA: Shaykh 'Abdul-'Azeez ibn Baaz (may Allah have Mercy on him) was asked the following question. Listen and summarize his answer in the box below.

Question: Can a traveler still break his fast even if he is using very comfortable means of transportation?

Shaykh Ibn Baaz replied:

عَنْ أَبِي سَعِيدٍ ــ رَضِيَ اللهُ عَنْهُ ــ : أَنَّ نَبِيَّ اللهِ ــ صَلَّى اللهُ عَلَيْهِ وَسَلَّمَ ــ قَالَ: «كَانَ فِيمَنْ كَانَ قَبْلَكُمْ رَجُلٌ قَتَلَ تِسْعَةً وَتِسْعِينَ نَفْسًا، فَسَأَلَ عَنْ أَعْلَمِ أَهْلِ الْأَرْضِ، فَدُلَّ عَلَى رَاهِبٍ، فَأَتَاهُ، فَقَالَ إِنَّهُ قَتَلَ تِسْعَةً وَتِسْعِينَ نَفْسًا، فَهَلْ لَهُ مِنْ تَوْبَةٍ؟ فَقَالَ: لَا، فَقَتَلَهُ، فَكَمَّلَ بِهِ مِائَةً! ثُمَّ سَأَلَ عَنْ أَعْلَمِ أَهْلِ الْأَرْضِ فَدُلَّ عَلَى رَجُلٍ عَالِمٍ، فَقَالَ: إِنَّهُ قَتَلَ مِائَةَ نَفْسٍ، فَهَلْ لَهُ مِنْ تَوْبَةٍ؟ فَقَالَ: نَعَمْ، وَمَنْ يَحُولُ بَيْنَهُ وَبَيْنَ التَّوْبَةِ؟ انْطَلِقْ إِلَى أَرْضِ كَذَا وَكَذَا، فَإِنَّ بِهَا أُنَاسًا يَعْبُدُونَ اللهَ، فَاعْبُدِ اللهَ مَعَهُمْ، وَلَا تَرْجِعْ إِلَى أَرْضِكَ، فَإِنَّهَا أَرْضُ سَوْءٍ، فَانْطَلَقَ حَتَّى إِذَا نَصَفَ الطَّرِيقَ أَتَاهُ الْمَوْتُ، فَاخْتَصَمَتْ فِيهِ مَلَائِكَةُ الرَّحْمَةِ وَمَلَائِكَةُ الْعَذَابِ، فَقَالَتْ مَلَائِكَةُ الرَّحْمَةِ: جَاءَ تَائِبًا مُقْبِلًا بِقَلْبِهِ إِلَى اللهِ، وَقَالَتْ مَلَائِكَةُ الْعَذَابِ: إِنَّهُ لَمْ يَعْمَلْ خَيْرًا قَطُّ، فَأَتَاهُمْ مَلَكٌ فِي صُورَةِ آدَمِيٍّ، فَجَعَلُوهُ بَيْنَهُمْ، فَقَالَ: قِيسُوا مَا بَيْنَ الْأَرْضَيْنِ، فَإِلَى أَيَّتِهِمَا كَانَ أَدْنَى فَهُوَ لَهُ، فَقَاسُوهُ فَوَجَدُوهُ أَدْنَى إِلَى الْأَرْضِ الَّتِي أَرَادَ، فَقَبَضَتْهُ مَلَائِكَةُ الرَّحْمَةِ.» (مُتَّفَقٌ عَلَيْهِ، وَهَذَا لَفْظُ مُسْلِمٍ)

On the authority of Aboo Sa'eed al-Khudree (may Allah be pleased with him), The Prophet of Allah (may Allah raise his rank and grant him peace) said: **There was a man from the Children of Israel before you who had killed 99 people. He asked for the most knowledgeable person in the land and was directed to a monk. He went to him, told him that he had killed 99 people, and asked if there was any way to repent. He replied, "No." So he killed him, completing 100 victims. He later asked again for the most knowledgeable person in the land and was directed to a knowledgeable person. He told him that he had killed 99 people, and asked if there was any way to repent. He replied, "Yes, and what would come between him and repentance?! Go to such-and-such land; there are people there worshipping Allah. Go worship Allah with them, and do not return to your land, because it is a land of evil." He set out until he was half-way there, at which point he died. So the Angels of mercy argued his case with the Angels of punishment. The Angels of mercy said, "He came repenting, turning to Allah with his heart." The Angels of punishment said, "He has not done any good deeds." So another Angel came in the form of a man to resolve their dispute. He said, "Measure the distance between the two lands, and whichever one he is closer to shall be the one he belongs to. They measured the distance, finding him closer to his destination, so the Angels of mercy took him.** (Agreed upon)

10.2 BENEFITS OF THE HADEETH

1) Aboo Sa'eed
2) "Agreed upon"
3) The harms of the ignorant and the virtue of the knowledgeable (Hadeeth)
4) Three types of souls: A) B) C)
5) Conditions to be fulfilled when repenting: A) B) C) D) When violating Allah's Right: Violating people's rights: E)
6) A confirmation of what was previously studied (4:97)
7) Connections to other hadeeth narrations (Hadeeth) (Hadeeth)
8) Not giving up hope in Allah's Mercy

9) Great news:

(20:82)

(13:6)

(42:25)

(Hadeeth)

10.3 FATWA: Shaykh 'Abdul-'Azeez ibn Baaz (may Allah have Mercy on him) was asked the following question. Listen and summarize his answer in the box below.

Question: Can a student break his fast during difficult final exams?

Shaykh Ibn Baaz replied:

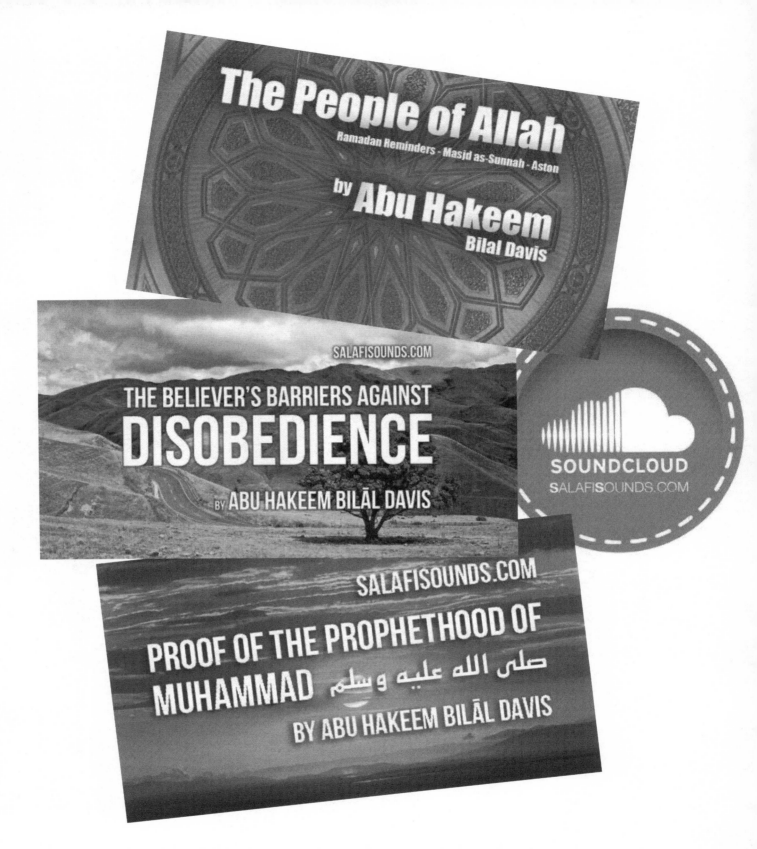

Your instructor highly recommends listening to the lectures and classes of Ustaadh Abu Hakeem Bilal Davis on the Soundcloud accounts of Masjid as-Sunnah Aston and SalafiSounds.

11.1 QURANIC PASSAGE & TRANSLATION

إِنَّمَا جَزَٰٓؤُاْ ٱلَّذِينَ يُحَارِبُونَ ٱللَّهَ وَرَسُولَهُۥ وَيَسْعَوْنَ فِي ٱلْأَرْضِ فَسَادًا أَن

يُقَتَّلُوٓاْ أَوْ يُصَلَّبُوٓاْ أَوْ تُقَطَّعَ أَيْدِيهِمْ وَأَرْجُلُهُم مِّنْ خِلَٰفٍ أَوْ يُنفَوْاْ مِنَ ٱلْأَرْضِ

ذَٰلِكَ لَهُمْ خِزْيٌ فِي ٱلدُّنْيَا وَلَهُمْ فِي ٱلْأَخِرَةِ عَذَابٌ عَظِيمٌ ٣٣ إِلَّا ٱلَّذِينَ تَابُواْ

مِن قَبْلِ أَن تَقْدِرُواْ عَلَيْهِمْ فَٱعْلَمُوٓاْ أَنَّ ٱللَّهَ غَفُورٌ رَّحِيمٌ ٣٤ (المائدة)

The only recompense for those who wage war against Allah and His Messenger and spread mischief throughout the land is to be killed, crucified, to have their hands and feet chopped off from opposite sides, or to be exiled from the land. That, for them, is a disgrace in this worldly life, and for them in the Hereafter is a severe punishment. Exempted are those who have repented before you capture them. And know that Allah is Oft-Forgiving, Ever-Merciful. (5:33-34)

11.2 TAFSEER BENEFITS

1) The incident about which the Verse was revealed (Hadeeth)
2) Differing over the four punishments A)   B)
3) Terrorists who kill and steal

4) Terrorists who steal (without killing)

5) Terrorists who threaten and scare people (without actually killing or stealing):

A)   B)

6) Scholarly differing over how/when the crucifixion is applied:

A)   B)

7) Scenario: A Muslim criminal comes to you and seeks your help, quoting a hadeeth:

(Hadeeth)

Correct course of action:

(5:2)

8) A disgrace in this life and a more severe punishment in the Next

9) The lofty status of those who combat such terrorism

10) Understanding the exemption

11) Two Names of Allah at the end of the Verse   *(Review: Module 5.2, Point #21)*

A)

B)

11.3 FATWA: Shaykh 'Abdul-'Azeez ibn Baaz (may Allah have Mercy on him) was asked the following question. Listen and summarize his answer in the box below.

Question: Is it permissible to get dental work done while fasting in Ramadhaan? What about local anesthetics?

Shaykh Ibn Baaz replied:

12.1 HADEETH & TRANSLATION

عَنْ أَنَسٍ _ رَضِيَ اللهِ عَنْهُ _ : أَنَّ نَاسًا مِنْ عُرَيْنَةَ قَدِمُوا عَلَى رَسُولِ اللهِ _ صَلَّى اللهُ عَلَيْهِ وَسَلَّمَ _ الْمَدِينَةَ، فَاجْتَوَوْهَا، فَقَالَ لَهُمْ رَسُولُ اللهِ _ صَلَّى اللهُ عَلَيْهِ وَسَلَّمَ _ : «إِنْ شِئْتُمْ أَنْ تَخْرُجُوا إِلَى إِبِلِ الصَّدَقَةِ، فَتَشْرَبُوا مِنْ أَلْبَانِهَا وَأَبْوَالِهَا»، فَفَعَلُوا، فَصَحُّوا، ثُمَّ مَالُوا عَلَى الرِّعَاءِ، فَقَتَلُوهُمْ وَارْتَدُّوا عَنِ الْإِسْلَامِ، وَسَاقُوا ذَوْدَ رَسُولِ اللهِ _ صَلَّى اللهُ عَلَيْهِ وَسَلَّمَ _ ، فَبَلَغَ ذَلِكَ النَّبِيَّ _ صَلَّى اللهُ عَلَيْهِ وَسَلَّمَ _ ، فَبَعَثَ فِي أَثَرِهِمْ، فَأُتِيَ بِهِمْ، فَقَطَعَ أَيْدِيَهُمْ وَأَرْجُلَهُمْ، وَسَمَلَ أَعْيُنَهُمْ، وَتَرَكَهُمْ فِي الْحَرَّةِ، حَتَّى مَاتُوا. (مُتَّفَقٌ عَلَيْهِ، وَهَذَا لَفْظُ مُسْلِمٍ)

On the authority of Anas (may Allah be pleased with him): Some people from the 'Uraynah Tribe came to the Messenger of Allah (may Allah raise his rank and grant him peace) in Madeenah. They became ill, so the Messenger of Allah (may Allah raise his rank and grant him peace) said, **"If you wish, go out to the camels collected from charity, and drink some of their milk and urine."** So they did that, and they regained their health. Then they all turned on the shepherds and killed them, abandoned Islam, and stole the camels of the Messenger of Allah (may Allah raise his rank and grant him peace). News of the event reached the Prophet (may Allah raise his rank and grant him peace), so he sent a search party after them, and then had their hands and feet chopped off and their eyes gouged out, and then he left them like that out in the valley until they died. (Agreed upon)

12.2 BENEFITS OF THE HADEETH

1) Anas
2) "Agreed upon"

49

3) "Some people from the 'Uraynah Tribe"
4) Why did they come to Madeenah?
5) Did he send them to the camel pen by themselves?
6) Why were their eyes gouged out?
7) Punishments of *qisaas* (retribution) on behalf of the deceased
8) *Qisaas* along with the death penalty
9) Were they really "waging war against Allah and His Messenger" like in the Verse? A) Aboo Qilaabah said: B) From what angle?
10) Were their limbs cauterized after the amputations?
11) Were some people kind to the terrorists as they were left to die? (24:2)
12) Should we protect our children from witnessing or hearing about such gore?
13) Those who say the urine of a camel is *najas* (filth) A *Fiqh* principle: (Hadeeth) (Hadeeth)
14) Responses to critics of Islam because of this medical treatment: A) B) C)

15) Responses to critics of Islam because of the harshness of this punishment:

A)

B)

C)

12.3 FATWA: Shaykh 'Abdul-'Azeez ibn Baaz (may Allah have Mercy on him) was asked the following question. Listen and summarize his answer in the box below.

Question: Can a fasting person use toothpaste, ear drops, nose drops, or eye drops? What if he can taste that in his throat?

Shaykh Ibn Baaz replied:

18 CONCISE BENEFITS FROM THE HADEETH OF JIBREEL

A FRIDAY KHUTBAH BY MOOSAA RICHARDSON

1439.05.23 (FEB 9, 2018)

Recommended recordings from our Spreaker channel

www.Spreaker.com/radio1mm

SHAYKH SAALIH AL-FOWZAAN
MAY ALLAAH PRESERVE HIM

Advice to the MUSLIMS Midway Through Ramadhaan 1437

TRANSLATED BY MOOSAA RICHARDSON

13.1 QURANIC PASSAGE & TRANSLATION

۞ وَعِندَهُۥ مَفَاتِحُ ٱلْغَيْبِ لَا يَعْلَمُهَآ إِلَّا هُوَ وَيَعْلَمُ مَا فِى ٱلْبَرِّ وَٱلْبَحْرِ وَمَا تَسْقُطُ مِن وَرَقَةٍ إِلَّا يَعْلَمُهَا وَلَا حَبَّةٍ فِى ظُلُمَٰتِ ٱلْأَرْضِ وَلَا رَطْبٍ وَلَا يَابِسٍ إِلَّا فِى كِتَٰبٍ مُّبِينٍ ۝ وَهُوَ ٱلَّذِى يَتَوَفَّىٰكُم بِٱلَّيْلِ وَيَعْلَمُ مَا جَرَحْتُم بِٱلنَّهَارِ ثُمَّ يَبْعَثُكُمْ فِيهِ لِيُقْضَىٰٓ أَجَلٌ مُّسَمًّى ثُمَّ إِلَيْهِ مَرْجِعُكُمْ ثُمَّ يُنَبِّئُكُم بِمَا كُنتُمْ تَعْمَلُونَ ۝ (الأنعام)

With Him are the keys of the Unseen, which no one knows other than Him. And He knows all that is on land and at sea. Not a single leaf falls except that He knows it, nor is there a single grain anywhere in the dark depths of the earth, and not a thing exists, moist or dry, except that it is in a clear written record. And He is the One who takes your souls by night, and He knows what actions you undertake throughout the day. He then sends you forth in it, so that a set term would be completed. Then, unto Him is your final return; and then, He informs you of all that you used to do. (6:59-60)

13.2 TAFSEER BENEFITS

1) Knowing all matters of the unseen is exclusive to Allah. (27:65)
2) Did the most knowledgeable of the Creation know all matters of the unseen? (6:50) (7:188)

3) The "Five Keys" of all unseen matters

(31:34)

(Hadeeth)

(Hadeeth)

4) The purpose of mentioning knowledge of the Unseen

5) "AND He knows all that is on land and at sea..."

6) All that is on land and at sea

7) A refutation of the *Mu'tazilah*

8) The clear written record

9) The ruling on someone who claims to have knowledge of the Unseen

Ibn 'Uthaymeen:

Al-Fowzaan:

10) The ruling on believing someone who claims to know the Unseen

(Hadeeth)

11) The ruling on listening to them while not believing them

(Hadeeth)

12) The ruling on the *Burdah* Poem and those who hold to its falsehood

(Ibn Baaz)

A recent local example:

13) The "lesser" taking of a soul (the lesser "death")   (3:55)   (42:42)
14) "...And He knows what actions you undertake throughout the day..."   (Ibn Katheer)
15) "Then He then sends you forth in IT..."   A.   B.
16) An important connection between the two types of "dying"   (Hadeeth)

Listen to the following important clarification:

https://www.spreaker.com/user/radio1mm/the-reality-of-the-sufi-spiritual-refine

13.3 ACTIVITY: Match the "Five Keys" as found in order in 31:34 to the "Five Keys" found in the Hadeeth of Ibn 'Umar in *Saheeh al-Bukhaaree*, as presented in today's lesson:

Quran 31:34	Hadeeth of Ibn 'Umar
1. *When is the Last Day?*	1. _____
2. _____	2. _____
3. _____	3. _____
4. _____	4. _____
5. _____	5. *When is the Last Day?*

13.4 FATWA: Shaykh 'Abdul-'Azeez ibn Baaz (may Allah have Mercy on him) was asked the following question. Listen and summarize his answer in the box below.

Question: Does vomiting break one's fast?

Shaykh Ibn Baaz replied:

56

HE CAME TO TEACH THE PEOPLE THEIR RELIGION

14.1 HADEETH & TRANSLATION

عَنْ أَبِي هُرَيْرَةَ ـ رَضِيَ اللهُ عَنْهُ ـ ، قَالَ: كَانَ النَّبِيُّ ـ صَلَّى اللهُ عَلَيْهِ وَسَلَّمَ ـ بَارِزًا يَوْمًا لِلنَّاسِ، فَأَتَاهُ جِبْرِيلُ، فَقَالَ: مَا الإِيْمَانُ؟ قَالَ: «الإِيْمَانُ أَنْ تُؤْمِنَ بِاللهِ، وَمَلاَئِكَتِهِ، وَكُتُبِهِ، وَبِلِقَائِهِ، وَرُسُلِهِ، وَتُؤْمِنَ بِالْبَعْثِ.» قَالَ: مَا الإِسْلاَمُ؟ قَالَ: «الإِسْلاَمُ: أَنْ تَعْبُدَ اللهَ وَلاَ تُشْرِكَ بِهِ شَيْئًا، وَتُقِيمَ الصَّلاَةَ، وَتُؤَدِّيَ الزَّكَاةَ الْمَفْرُوضَةَ، وَتَصُومَ رَمَضَانَ.» قَالَ: مَا الإِحْسَانُ؟ قَالَ: «أَنْ تَعْبُدَ اللهَ كَأَنَّكَ تَرَاهُ، فَإِنْ لَمْ تَكُنْ تَرَاهُ فَإِنَّهُ يَرَاكَ.» قَالَ: مَتَى السَّاعَةُ؟ قَالَ: «مَا الْمَسْئُولُ عَنْهَا بِأَعْلَمَ مِنَ السَّائِلِ؛ وَسَأُخْبِرُكَ عَنْ أَشْرَاطِهَا: إِذَا وَلَدَتِ الأَمَةُ رَبَّهَا، وَإِذَا تَطَاوَلَ رُعَاةُ الإِبِلِ الْبُهْمُ فِي الْبُنْيَانِ، فِي خَمْسٍ لاَ يَعْلَمُهُنَّ إِلَّا اللهُ، ثُمَّ تَلاَ النَّبِيُّ ـ صَلَّى اللهُ عَلَيْهِ وَسَلَّمَ ـ: {إِنَّ اللهَ عِنْدَهُ عِلْمُ السَّاعَةِ} الآيَةَ، ثُمَّ أَدْبَرَ، فَقَالَ: «رُدُّوهُ!» فَلَمْ يَرَوْا شَيْئًا، فَقَالَ: «هَذَا جِبْرِيلُ، جَاءَ يُعَلِّمُ النَّاسَ دِينَهُمْ.» (مُتَّفَقٌ عَلَيْهِ)

On the authority of Aboo Hurayrah (may Allah be pleased with him): The Prophet (may Allah raise his rank and grant him peace) was out with the people one day, when Jibreel arrived. He asked, "What is *eemaan*?" He said, "**Eemaan is to believe in Allah, His Angels, His Books, His Meeting, His Messengers, and to believe in the Resurrection.**" He then asked, "What is Islam?" He replied, "**Islam is that you worship Allah without worshipping anyone beside Him, establish prayers, pay the obligatory *Zakaat*, and fast in Ramadhaan.**" He asked, "What is *ihsaan*?" He replied, "**That you worship Allah as if you can see Him; while you do not see Him, He does see you.**" He asked, "When is the Hour?" He replied, "**The one being asked knows no more than the questioner, but I will inform you of its signs: When a slave-girl gives birth to her master, and when the destitute camel shepherds compete in building tall buildings, amid five things known only to Allah...**" Then the Prophet (may Allah raise his rank and grant him peace) recited: "**Verily, Allah Alone has knowledge of the Hour,**" the Verse. Then, he left. He said, "**Bring him back.**" Yet they did not see anyone at all. He said, "**That was Jibreel; he came to teach the people their Religion.**" (Agreed upon)

14.2 BENEFITS OF THE HADEETH

1) Aboo Hurayrah
2) "Agreed upon"
3) Isn't the hadeeth of Jibreel narrated by 'Umar?
4) "when Jibreel arrived"
5) Where is the mention of *Hajj* and *Qadr*?
6) Two things not mentioned in the version of 'Umar: A.   B.
7) We studied the hadeeth of Jibreel at 1MM over eight months.

14.3 FATWA: Shaykh 'Abdul-'Azeez ibn Baaz (may Allah have Mercy on him) was asked the following question. Listen and summarize his answer in the box below.

Question: How can one repent from masturbation during one's fast?

Shaykh Ibn Baaz replied:

15.1 QURANIC PASSAGE & TRANSLATION

۞ قُلْ تَعَالَوْا۟ أَتْلُ مَا حَرَّمَ رَبُّكُمْ عَلَيْكُمْ أَلَّا تُشْرِكُوا۟ بِهِۦ شَيْـًٔا وَبِٱلْوَٰلِدَيْنِ إِحْسَٰنًا وَلَا تَقْتُلُوٓا۟ أَوْلَٰدَكُم مِّنْ إِمْلَٰقٍ نَّحْنُ نَرْزُقُكُمْ وَإِيَّاهُمْ وَلَا تَقْرَبُوا۟ ٱلْفَوَٰحِشَ مَا ظَهَرَ مِنْهَا وَمَا بَطَنَ وَلَا تَقْتُلُوا۟ ٱلنَّفْسَ ٱلَّتِى حَرَّمَ ٱللَّهُ إِلَّا بِٱلْحَقِّ ذَٰلِكُمْ وَصَّىٰكُم بِهِۦ لَعَلَّكُمْ تَعْقِلُونَ ۝ وَلَا تَقْرَبُوا۟ مَالَ ٱلْيَتِيمِ إِلَّا بِٱلَّتِى هِىَ أَحْسَنُ حَتَّىٰ يَبْلُغَ أَشُدَّهُۥ وَأَوْفُوا۟ ٱلْكَيْلَ وَٱلْمِيزَانَ بِٱلْقِسْطِ لَا نُكَلِّفُ نَفْسًا إِلَّا وُسْعَهَا وَإِذَا قُلْتُمْ فَٱعْدِلُوا۟ وَلَوْ كَانَ ذَا قُرْبَىٰ وَبِعَهْدِ ٱللَّهِ أَوْفُوا۟ ذَٰلِكُمْ وَصَّىٰكُم بِهِۦ لَعَلَّكُمْ تَذَكَّرُونَ ۝ وَأَنَّ هَٰذَا صِرَٰطِى مُسْتَقِيمًا فَٱتَّبِعُوهُ وَلَا تَتَّبِعُوا۟ ٱلسُّبُلَ فَتَفَرَّقَ بِكُمْ عَن سَبِيلِهِۦ ذَٰلِكُمْ وَصَّىٰكُم بِهِۦ لَعَلَّكُمْ تَتَّقُونَ ۝ (الأنعام)

Say: Come, let me recite unto you what your Lord has made impermissible for you: That you not ascribe partners to Him in worship, that you be kind to parents, and that you do not kill your children out of poverty. We provide for you and them. And do not approach obscenities, whether openly committed or hidden. And do not kill any soul which Allah has forbidden, except by right. That is what Allah admonishes you with, in order for you to use your intellect. And do not come near the orphan's wealth, except with what is better, until he reaches the age of full strength. And measure out your weights and measures fairly. We do not burden any soul beyond its ability. And when you speak, be just, even if it be against a close relative. And Allah's covenant is something you must uphold! That is what He admonishes you with, in order for you to reflect. And this is My straight Path, so follow it. And do not follow the other paths, as they will land you in discord, away from His Path. That is what He admonishes you with, in order for you to attain piety. (6:151-153)

15.2 TAFSEER BENEFITS

1) Who was this Verse originally addressed to? (7:28-32)
2) Messengers reciting Allah's Verses upon the people (39:71) (28:59)
3) "What your Lord has made impermissible for you"
4) The first and foremost of the ten admonitions
5) Kindness to parents [#2 of 10]
6) The prohibition of killing one's children in poverty [#3 of 10] A logical deduction:
7) Provisions are set and guaranteed
8) "And do not approach obscenities" [#4 of 10]
9) The prohibition of murder [#5 of 10]
10) Taking a life "by right" ?? (Hadeeth)
11) "That is what Allah admonishes you with, in order for you to use your intellect"
12) An orphan's inheritance is protected in Islam [#6 of 10]
13) Fairness and precision in weights and measures [#7 of 10] (55:9) (83:1-4)

14) Allah reminds us of His Fairness in Legislation
15) A principle in Islamic Legal Maxims
16) An amazing reminder at this specific point
17) Fairness and impartiality in speech and testimony [#8 of 10]
18) Upholding covenants [#9 of 10] A. B.
19) "That is what He admonishes you with, in order for you to reflect"
20) Bringing all this together in a comprehensive summary
21) The order to follow, in unity, and not be divided [#10 of 10]
22) "That is what He admonishes you with, in order for you to attain piety"
23) One single path of Truth vs. multiple paths of deviation   *(Review Lesson 15 from Volume 1)*
24) Making connections: How the three Verses end (6:151) (6:152) (6:153)
25) Making connections: *Soorah al-Faatihah*

15.3 RESEARCH: The scholars mention that these three Verses (6:151-153) also contain five basic human necessities that have always been safeguarded for the people in every divine message. Summarize them in the table below:

FIVE BASIC HUMAN RIGHTS AS FOUND IN 6:151-153	
1	
2	
3	
4	
5	

❁ For help on the topic, refer to the following brief article:

The Five Basic Human Rights (Or Essentials) Islaam Safeguards and Honors

15.4 FATWA: Shaykh 'Abdul-'Azeez ibn Baaz (may Allah have Mercy on him) was asked the following question. Listen and summarize his answer in the box below.

Question: Does a nosebleed break someone's fast? What about donating blood or having blood drawn for medical tests?

Shaykh Ibn Baaz replied:

16.1 HADEETH & TRANSLATION

عَنْ عَبْدِ اللهِ بْنِ مَسْعُودٍ ــ رَضِيَ اللهُ عَنْهُ ــ ، قَالَ: خَطَّ لَنَا رَسُولُ اللهِ ــ صَلَّى اللهُ عَلَيْهِ وَسَلَّمَ ــ خَطًّا، ثُمَّ قَالَ: «هَذَا سَبِيلُ اللهِ»، ثُمَّ خَطَّ خُطُوطًا عَنْ يَمِينِهِ وَعَنْ شِمَالِهِ، ثُمَّ قَالَ: «هَذِهِ سُبُلٌ مُتَفَرِّقَةٌ، عَلَى كُلِّ سَبِيلٍ مِنْهَا شَيْطَانٌ يَدْعُو إِلَيْهِ»، ثُمَّ قَرَأَ: ﴿ وَأَنَّ هَذَا صِرَاطِي مُسْتَقِيمًا فَاتَّبِعُوهُ وَلَا تَتَّبِعُوا السُّبُلَ فَتَفَرَّقَ بِكُمْ عَنْ سَبِيلِهِ ﴾ . (أَخْرَجَهُ أَحْمَدُ وَابْنُ حِبَّانَ)

On the authority of 'Abdullaah ibn Mas'ood (may Allah be pleased with him), who said: The Messenger of Allah (may Allah raise his rank and grant him peace) drew a line for us, and then he said: **"This is the Path of Allah."** Then, he drew lines to the right and left of it, and said: **"These are differing paths, upon each of them is a devil calling to it."** Then he recited, **"And this is My straight Path, so follow it. And do not follow the other paths, as they will land you in discord, away from His Path."** (Ahmad, Ibn Hibbaan)

16.2 BENEFITS OF THE HADEETH

1) 'Abdullaah ibn Mas'ood
2) Ahmad ibn Hanbal
3) Ibn Hibbaan
4) Ibrahim's supplication and Allah's Response (2:127-129)   (3:164)

5) How the *Sunnah* explains the *Thikr* (16:44)
6) Visual aids in teaching
7) Confirming the 23rd point from the *Tafseer* benefits of the previous lesson
8) The obligation of unity upon the Book & *Sunnah* (3:102-105)   (6:159)
9) The decreed division of the *Ummah* into 73 sects

16.3 FATWA: Shaykh 'Abdul-'Azeez ibn Baaz (may Allah have Mercy on him) was asked the following question. Listen and summarize his answer in the box below.

Question: What is the ruling on using prayer schedules that include an "imsaak" time before Fajr?

Shaykh Ibn Baaz replied:

TRUE BELIEVERS DESCRIBED IN DETAIL

17.1 QURANIC PASSAGE & TRANSLATION

﴿ يَسْـَٔلُونَكَ عَنِ ٱلْأَنفَالِ قُلِ ٱلْأَنفَالُ لِلَّهِ وَٱلرَّسُولِ فَٱتَّقُوا۟ ٱللَّهَ وَأَصْلِحُوا۟ ذَاتَ بَيْنِكُمْ وَأَطِيعُوا۟ ٱللَّهَ وَرَسُولَهُۥٓ إِن كُنتُم مُّؤْمِنِينَ ۝ إِنَّمَا ٱلْمُؤْمِنُونَ ٱلَّذِينَ إِذَا ذُكِرَ ٱللَّهُ وَجِلَتْ قُلُوبُهُمْ وَإِذَا تُلِيَتْ عَلَيْهِمْ ءَايَٰتُهُۥ زَادَتْهُمْ إِيمَٰنًا وَعَلَىٰ رَبِّهِمْ يَتَوَكَّلُونَ ۝ ٱلَّذِينَ يُقِيمُونَ ٱلصَّلَوٰةَ وَمِمَّا رَزَقْنَٰهُمْ يُنفِقُونَ ۝ أُو۟لَٰٓئِكَ هُمُ ٱلْمُؤْمِنُونَ حَقًّا ۚ لَّهُمْ دَرَجَٰتٌ عِندَ رَبِّهِمْ وَمَغْفِرَةٌ وَرِزْقٌ كَرِيمٌ ۝ ﴾ (الأنفال)

They ask you about the spoils of war. Say: 'The spoils of war are the right of Allah and His Messenger, so fear Allah and rectify whatever is between yourselves, and obey Allah and His Messenger if you are indeed believers.' The believers are only those who, when Allah is mentioned, their hearts tremble in fear, and when His Verses are recited unto them, they are increased in faith, and they place their trust solely upon their Lord. [They are] those who establish prayer and spend from what We have provided them with. Those are the ones who are believers in truth; for them are levels [of reward] with their Lord, Forgiveness, and generous provisions. (8:1-4)

17.2 TAFSEER BENEFITS

1) The meaning of the word *"Anfaal"*
2) The incident about which these Verses were revealed
3) Verses with: "They ask you about such-and-such..."

4) "The spoils of war are the right of Allah and His Messenger"

5) The order to have *taqwa* and its general meaning

6) The order to bring about rectification in matters of differing

7) The order to obey Allah and His Messenger

8) "The believers are only those who..."

9) Hearts that tremble at the mention of Allah

10) Faith increased by hearing the Verses recited

11) *Tawakkul* – placing one's trust solely upon Allah

12) The establishment of the prayer

13) Spending from Allah's provisions

14) Such people are the true believers

15) An observation about the order of the behaviors mentioned

16) *Eemaan* (faith) fluctuates	
17) Three great rewards:	
18) The exclusive nature of this reward	

17.3 ACTIVITY: Summarize the five attributes of the true believers mentioned by Allah in the second and third Verses of *Soorah al-Anfaal*:

ATTRIBUTES OF TRUE BELIEVERS FROM QURAN (8:2-3)	
1	*Their hearts tremble at the mention of Allah*
2	
3	
4	
5	

17.4 RESEARCH: Building on the narration of Ibn 'Abbaas that we studied, that there are 13 occasions when the Companions asked about topics, locate the passages in the Quran wherein Allah says [what means]: *"They ask you about such-and-such…"* and list them below:

VERSES WITH: "THEY ASK YOU ABOUT…"		
1	2 : 189	*The crescent moons, the lunar months*
2		
3		
4		

5		
6		
7		
8		
9		
10		
11		
12		
13		

17.5 FATWA: Shaykh 'Abdul-'Azeez ibn Baaz (may Allah have Mercy on him) was asked the following question. Listen and summarize his answer in the box below.

Question: Is a man's fast valid if he slept past the time for suhoor and only woke up after Fajr had entered?

Shaykh Ibn Baaz replied:

18.1 HADEETH & TRANSLATION

عَنْ أَبِي هُرَيْرَةَ ــ رَضِيَ اللهُ عَنْهُ ــ، قَالَ: قَالَ رَسُولُ اللهِ ــ صَلَّى اللهُ عَلَيْهِ
وَسَلَّمَ ــ: «سَبْعَةٌ يُظِلُّهُمُ اللهُ تَعَالَى فِي ظِلِّهِ يَوْمَ لاَ ظِلَّ إِلَّا ظِلُّهُ: إِمَامٌ عَدْلٌ،
وَشَابٌّ نَشَأَ فِي عِبَادَةِ اللهِ، وَرَجُلٌ قَلْبُهُ مُعَلَّقٌ فِي المَسَاجِدِ، وَرَجُلاَنِ تَحَابَّا فِي
اللهِ اجْتَمَعَا عَلَيْهِ وَتَفَرَّقَا عَلَيْهِ، وَرَجُلٌ دَعَتْهُ امْرَأَةٌ ذَاتُ مَنْصِبٍ وَجَمَالٍ، فَقَالَ:
إِنِّي أَخَافُ اللهَ، وَرَجُلٌ تَصَدَّقَ بِصَدَقَةٍ فَأَخْفَاهَا حَتَّى لاَ تَعْلَمَ شِمَالُهُ مَا تُنْفِقُ
يَمِينُهُ، وَرَجُلٌ ذَكَرَ اللهَ خَالِيًا، فَفَاضَتْ عَيْنَاهُ.» (مُتَّفَقٌ عَلَيْهِ)

On the authority of Aboo Hurayrah (may Allah be pleased with him): The Messenger of Allah (may Allah raise his rank and grant him peace) said, **"Seven shall be shaded by Allah, the Most High, in His Shade, on the Day when there shall be no shade other than His: [1] A just leader, [2] a young man raised in the worship of Allah, [3] a man whose heart is attached to the masjids, [4] two men who love one another for Allah's sake, coming together and parting for that only, [5] a man invited by a woman of beauty and lineage, who says: "Rather, I am afraid of Allah," [6] a man who gives in charity so secretly that his own left hand does not know how much his right has given, [7] and a man who remembers Allah in seclusion and his eyes pour out tears."** (Agreed upon)

18.2 BENEFITS OF THE HADEETH

1) Aboo Hurayrah
2) Agreed upon

3) Seven individual people or seven types of people?

4) Pondering over a special blessing from Allah

5) What is this shade mentioned?

(Hadeeth)

(Hadeeth)

(Hadeeth)

6) The just leader

(Hadeeth)

(Hadeeth)

7) A young man raised in the worship of Allah

8) Two-way benefits of raising Muslim children:

(52:21)

(Athar)

9) Hearts connected to the Houses of Allah

(24:36-37)

10) Allah has made it easy to love the masjids.

(Hadeeth)

11) Believers loving one another for Allah's Sake

(Hadeeth)

(Hadeeth)

12) Refusing obscene invitations (17:32) (23:1-7)
13) Giving charity in secret (2:271) (Hadeeth)
14) Weeping out of the fear of Allah (19:58) (Hadeeth)
15) The excellence of worship done in secret (Hadeeth)
16) The mention of men (males) throughout this hadeeth (16:97)

18.3 FROM YOUR MEMORY: Try to list all seven people under the shade, according to the hadeeth we studied. Go back and fill in the ones you did not remember afterwards.

THE SEVEN PEOPLE UNDER THE SHADE OF ALLAH'S THRONE	
1	
2	
3	
4	
5	
6	
7	

18.4 FATWA: Shaykh 'Abdul-'Azeez ibn Baaz (may Allah have Mercy on him) was asked the following question. Listen and summarize his answer in the box below.

Question: What does a fasting person do when his plane travels to the West and the sun does not set for many more hours than he expected?

Shaykh Ibn Baaz replied:

19.1 QURANIC PASSAGE & TRANSLATION

وَالْمُؤْمِنُونَ وَالْمُؤْمِنَتُ بَعْضُهُمْ أَوْلِيَاءُ بَعْضٍ يَأْمُرُونَ بِالْمَعْرُوفِ وَيَنْهَوْنَ عَنِ الْمُنكَرِ وَيُقِيمُونَ الصَّلَوٰةَ وَيُؤْتُونَ الزَّكَوٰةَ وَيُطِيعُونَ اللَّهَ وَرَسُولَهُۥ أُولَٰئِكَ سَيَرْحَمُهُمُ اللَّهُ إِنَّ اللَّهَ عَزِيزٌ حَكِيمٌ ۝ وَعَدَ اللَّهُ الْمُؤْمِنِينَ وَالْمُؤْمِنَتِ جَنَّتٍ تَجْرِي مِن تَحْتِهَا الْأَنْهَٰرُ خَٰلِدِينَ فِيهَا وَمَسَٰكِنَ طَيِّبَةً فِي جَنَّتِ عَدْنٍ وَرِضْوَٰنٌ مِّنَ اللَّهِ أَكْبَرُ ذَٰلِكَ هُوَ الْفَوْزُ الْعَظِيمُ ۝ (التوبة)

The believing men and believing women are allies to one another; they enjoin good, forbid evil, establish prayer, pay *zakaat***, and obey Allah and His Messenger. Such are those whom Allah has Mercy on. Verily, Allah is All-Mighty, Ever Wise. Allah has promised the believing men and believing women gardens under which rivers flow, abiding therein forever, and fine dwelling places amid gardens of eternal joy. And the Pleasure of Allah is even greater; that is the great success.** (9:71-72)

19.2 TAFSEER BENEFITS

1) A comparative look at two Verses about the hypocrites (9:67) (9:68)
2) "The believing men and the believing women..."

73

3) Believers are allies to one another   (Hadeeth)

4) A deviant modern explanation of this Verse
 	
   (And 49:13)
 	
   The response:

5) The first description of believers who are allies by faith
 	
   (3:104)
 	
   (Hadeeth)

6) The establishment of prayer
7) The payment of *zakaat*

8) Obedience to Allah and His Messenger
 	
   (4:64)
 	
   (4:80)
 	
   (8:1)

9) Special Mercy for devout worshippers
 	
   (3:132)
 	
   (8:56)
 	
   (49:10)

10) A subtle indication implied   (Hadeeth)

11) Effects of enjoining and forbidding vs. abandoning that for "unity"

(Hadeeth)

(Hadeeth)

12) The two Names of Allah: *al-'Azeez* and *al-Hakeem*

Al-'Azeez:

Al-Hakeem:

When combined:

13) Another confirmation of gender equality in Religious matters

14) "Fine dwelling places amid gardens of eternal joy…"

15) "And the Pleasure of Allah is even greater…"

(Hadeeth)

16) The great success compared to the great loss

(9:68)

19.3 FATWA: Shaykh 'Abdul-'Azeez ibn Baaz (may Allah have Mercy on him) was asked the following question. Listen and summarize his answer in the box below.

Question: What does a person do if he broke his fast because it was difficult? What if that was many years ago?

Shaykh Ibn Baaz replied:

FOCUSING ON YOURSELF PRIMARILY, NOT EXCLUSIVELY

20.1 HADEETH STUDY

عَنْ قَيْسِ بْنِ أَبِي حَازِمٍ، قَالَ: قَالَ أَبُو بَكْرٍ ــ رَضِيَ اللهُ عَنْهُ ــ بَعْدَ أَنْ حَمِدَ اللهَ،

وَأَثْنَى عَلَيْهِ: يَا أَيُّهَا النَّاسُ! إِنَّكُمْ تَقْرَؤُونَ هَذِهِ الآيَةَ وَتَضَعُونَهَا عَلَى غَيْرِ مَوَاضِعِهَا:

﴿يَٰٓأَيُّهَا ٱلَّذِينَ ءَامَنُوا۟ عَلَيْكُمْ أَنفُسَكُمْ لَا يَضُرُّكُم مَّن ضَلَّ إِذَا ٱهْتَدَيْتُمْ﴾ [المَائِدَة: ١٠٥]،

وَإِنِّي سَمِعْتُ رَسُولَ اللهِ ــ صَلَّى اللهُ عَلَيْهِ وَسَلَّمَ ــ يَقُولُ: «مَا مِنْ قَوْمٍ يُعْمَلُ

فِيهِمْ بِالمَعَاصِي، ثُمَّ يَقْدِرُونَ عَلَى أَنْ يُغَيِّرُوا، ثُمَّ لَا يُغَيِّرُوا، إِلَّا يُوشِكُ أَنْ يَعُمَّهُمُ

اللهُ مِنْهُ بِعِقَابٍ.» (أَخْرَجَهُ أَبُو دَاوُدَ وَاللَّفْظُ لَهُ، وَالتِّرْمِذِيُّ، وَقَالَ: حَسَنٌ صَحِيحٌ)

Qays ibn Abee Haazim reported that Aboo Bakr (may Allah be pleased with him) once praised Allah and extolled him, and then said: "O people! You are reciting this Verse and you are putting it in other than its proper places (of implementation): **'O you who believe! Upon you is your own selves; none of those who stray shall harm you if you are rightly guided.'** [5:105] Indeed, I did hear the Messenger of Allah (may Allah raise his rank and grant him peace) saying: **'There are no people among whom disobedience is done** (widely), **while they are capable of changing it, yet they do not change it, except that Allah is about to cover them all with a punishment from Himself!'"** (Aboo Daawood, at-Tirmithee)

20.2 BENEFITS OF THE HADEETH

1) Qays ibn Abee Haazim
2) Aboo Bakr
3) Aboo Daawood

4) At-Tirmithee

5) A stern warning of an all-compassing punishment

(At-Tirmithee's chapter title)

(8:25)

6) Ordering and forbidding is naseehah

(Hadeeth)

7) The three levels of forbidding evil

(Hadeeth)

8) Another terrible result of leaving off enjoining and forbidding

(5:77-79)

9) So then what is the meaning of "Upon you is your own selves..."

10) Real life examples of failure to implement the Verse

11) "Allah is **about to** cover them..."

12) The lofty status of Aboo Bakr and his era of leadership

13) The arrival of ignorance and misunderstandings early in the *Ummah*

14) An example of *Tafseer* of Quran by Sunnah, as done by a Companion

15) Is this all-encompassing punishment a worldly one? Or in the Hereafter?

A.

B.

(Hadeeth)

20.3 FATWA: Shaykh 'Abdul-'Azeez ibn Baaz (may Allah have Mercy on him) was asked the following question. Listen and summarize his answer in the box below.

Question: If someone broke his fast for two days in a row with a valid excuse, must he make up those two days consecutively?

Shaykh Ibn Baaz replied:

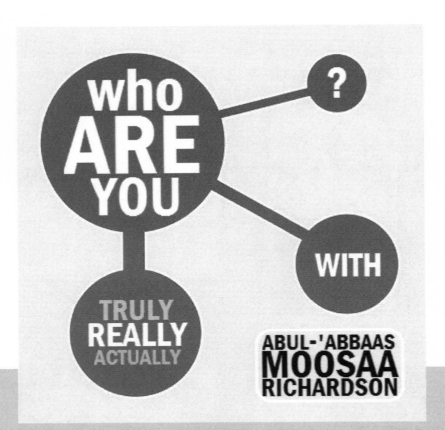

Recommended recordings from our Spreaker channel

www.Spreaker.com/radio1mm

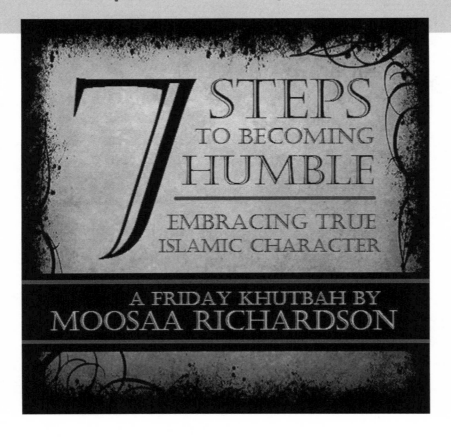

21.1 QURANIC PASSAGE & TRANSLATION

قُل يَٰٓأَيُّهَا ٱلنَّاسُ إِن كُنتُمۡ فِى شَكٍّ مِّن دِينِى فَلَآ أَعۡبُدُ ٱلَّذِينَ تَعۡبُدُونَ مِن دُونِ ٱللَّهِ

وَلَٰكِنۡ أَعۡبُدُ ٱللَّهَ ٱلَّذِى يَتَوَفَّىٰكُمۡ وَأُمِرۡتُ أَنۡ أَكُونَ مِنَ ٱلۡمُؤۡمِنِينَ ۝ وَأَنۡ أَقِمۡ وَجۡهَكَ

لِلدِّينِ حَنِيفًا وَلَا تَكُونَنَّ مِنَ ٱلۡمُشۡرِكِينَ ۝ وَلَا تَدۡعُ مِن دُونِ ٱللَّهِ مَا لَا يَنفَعُكَ وَلَا

يَضُرُّكَ فَإِن فَعَلۡتَ فَإِنَّكَ إِذًا مِّنَ ٱلظَّٰلِمِينَ ۝ وَإِن يَمۡسَسۡكَ ٱللَّهُ بِضُرٍّ فَلَا كَاشِفَ

لَهُۥ إِلَّا هُوَ وَإِن يُرِدۡكَ بِخَيۡرٍ فَلَا رَآدَّ لِفَضۡلِهِۦ يُصِيبُ بِهِۦ مَن يَشَآءُ مِنۡ عِبَادِهِۦ وَهُوَ

ٱلۡغَفُورُ ٱلرَّحِيمُ ۝ ﴿ (يونس)

Say: O Mankind! If you are in doubt about my Religion, then I do not worship those besides Allah whom you worship. Rather, I worship Allah, the One who takes your souls. I have been ordered to be among the believers, and that you set your face to the Religion as a monotheist, and that you must not ever be one of the polytheists. And do not call upon those beside Allah, those who do not benefit you nor harm you. If you do, then certainly you would be among the oppressors. Whenever Allah causes harm to reach you, none can remove it other than Him Alone. Whenever He wants good for you, none can block His Favor; He gives it to whomsoever He wills of His servants. And Allah is Oft-Forgiving, the Ever Merciful. (10:104-107)

21.2 TAFSEER BENEFITS

1) An order to a Prophet is an order to his followers
2) Islam is a universal message to all of humanity. (7:158) (34:28)
3) "If you are in doubt about my Religion..."
4) I do not worship what you worship (109:1-6)
5) Repeated patterns throughout human history (11:62-63) (14:9-10)
6) "I worship Allah, the One who takes your souls..."
7) "I have been ordered to be among the believers"
8) "And that you set your face to the Religion as a monotheist..."
9) "And that you must not ever be one of the polytheists..."
10) "And do not call upon those beside Allah who do not benefit you or harm you..."

11) "If you do, then certainly you would be among the oppressors..." (31:13)
12) True believers are afraid of committing polytheism (39:65-66)
13) No one can repel a harm which Allah has decreed
14) No one can prevent Allah's Favor which He has decreed for someone (35:2)
15) "He gives it to whomsoever He wills of His servants..." (3:73-74)
16) Allah is the Oft-Forgiving
17) Allah is the Ever Merciful

21.3 FATWA: Shaykh 'Abdul-'Azeez ibn Baaz (may Allah have Mercy on him) was asked the following question. Listen and summarize his answer in the box below.

Question: How does a person repent and rectify his affair after years of neglecting prayers and fasting?

Shaykh Ibn Baaz replied:

21.4 RESEARCH: Locate and summarize 21 Quranic passages wherein Allah addresses Mankind using the phrase, *"Yaa Ayyuhan-Naas"* (*O Mankind!*), or He commands one of His Prophets to do so. **NOTE:** The first seven passages are cited for you. The following eight passages are from *Soorah Yoonus* and *Soorah al-Hajj*. Also, note that 4:133 does not have the complete phrase, yet it is *muqaddar* (understood to be there, based on context).

QURANIC VERSES WITH: *"YAA AYYUHAN-NAAS..."* (O PEOPLE/MANKIND...)		
1	2 : 21	Worship your Lord who created you, so you might attain piety
2	2 : 168	
3	4 : 1	
4	4 : 133	
5	4 : 170	
6	4 : 174	
7	7 : 158	
8	10 :	
9	10 :	
10	10 :	
11	10 :	
12	22 :	
13	22 :	
14	22 :	
15	22 :	
16		
17		
18		
19		
20		
21		

OBEDIENCE TO ALLAH & TRUE RELIANCE UPON HIM

22.1 HADEETH STUDY

عَنِ ابْنِ عَبَّاسٍ ــ رَضِيَ اللهُ عَنْهُمَا ــ ، قَالَ: كُنْتُ خَلْفَ رَسُولِ اللهِ ــ صَلَّى اللهُ عَلَيْهِ وَسَلَّمَ ــ يَوْمًا، فَقَالَ: «يَا غُلَامُ! إِنِّي أُعَلِّمُكَ كَلِمَاتٍ: احْفَظِ اللهَ يَحْفَظْكَ؛ احْفَظِ اللهَ تَجِدْهُ تُجَاهَكَ؛ إِذَا سَأَلْتَ فَاسْأَلِ اللهَ، وَإِذَا اسْتَعَنْتَ فَاسْتَعِنْ بِاللهِ. وَاعْلَمْ أَنَّ الْأُمَّةَ لَوِ اجْتَمَعَتْ عَلَى أَنْ يَنْفَعُوكَ بِشَيْءٍ لَمْ يَنْفَعُوكَ إِلَّا بِشَيْءٍ قَدْ كَتَبَهُ اللهُ لَكَ، وَلَوِ اجْتَمَعُوا عَلَى أَنْ يَضُرُّوكَ بِشَيْءٍ لَمْ يَضُرُّوكَ إِلَّا بِشَيْءٍ قَدْ كَتَبَهُ اللهُ عَلَيْكَ؛ رُفِعَتِ الْأَقْلَامُ، وَجَفَّتِ الصُّحُفُ.» (أَخْرَجَهُ التِّرْمِذِيُّ، وَقَالَ: حَسَنٌ صَحِيحٌ)

On the authority of Ibn 'Abbaas (may Allah be pleased with him and his father), who said: I was behind the Messenger of Allah (may Allah raise his rank and grant him peace) one day, and he said: **"O young man! I am going to teach you some words: Preserve Allah; He will preserve you. Preserve Allah; you will find Him in front of you. Whenever you ask, ask Allah, and whenever you seek help, seek Allah's Help. Know that if the entire population were to come together to benefit you with something, they would not benefit you with anything other than what Allah had already written for you. And if they all came together to harm you with something, they would not harm you with anything other than what Allah has already written to befall you. The pens have been lifted; the pages have dried."** (At-Tirmithee)

22.2 BENEFITS OF THE HADEETH

1) Ibn 'Abbaas
2) At-Tirmithee
3) The significance of this hadeeth
4) "I was behind the Messenger..."
5) "O young man! I am going to teach you some words..."
6) The meaning of "preserving Allah" (50:32-33)
7) Recompense is similar to the deed performed. (2:40) (2:152) (47:7)
8) Allah preserves people in both worldly and religious ways A) In worldly matters: (13:11) B) In Religious matters: (8:24)
9) "You will find Him in front of you..." (16:128)
10) Asking Allah alone (1:5) (Hadeeth)

(Hadeeth)

11) Supplicating to Allah is a Religious obligation.

(4:32)

(Hadeeth)

(Hadeeth)

12) Asking other than Allah is of two main categories:

A)

(23:117)

B) Asking people for things not exclusive to Allah:

i)

ii)

(5:2)

iii)

(Hadeeth)

iv)

(Hadeeth)

(Hadeeth)

(Hadeeth)

13) "Know that if the entire population were to come together..."

14) "The pens have been lifted; the pages have dried."

(Hadeeth)

15) Many benefits of Muslim belief in *Qadr*

22.3 ACTIVITY: Memorize and/or rehearse the supplication found in an authentic hadeeth collected by Imaam at-Tirmithee and others, when 'Aa'ishah asked what she should say if she caught *Laytal-Qadr*. The Prophet (may Allah raise his rank and grant him peace) instructed her to supplicate:

«اللّهُمَّ إِنَّكَ عَفُوٌّ، تُحِبُّ الْعَفْوَ، فَاعْفُ عَنِّي!»

"O Allah! Certainly, You are the One who pardons;
You love to pardon, so pardon me!"

22.4 FATWA: Shaykh 'Abdul-'Azeez ibn Baaz (may Allah have Mercy on him) was asked the following question. Listen and summarize his answer in the box below.

Question: A woman who always fasts six days in Shawwaal could not do so one year because she had a baby that Ramadhaan. Can she make up the days from Shawwaal later, after she makes up for her days from Ramadhaan?

Shaykh Ibn Baaz replied:

23.1 QURANIC PASSAGE & TRANSLATION

فَٱسْتَقِمْ كَمَآ أُمِرْتَ وَمَن تَابَ مَعَكَ وَلَا تَطْغَوْا۟ إِنَّهُۥ بِمَا تَعْمَلُونَ بَصِيرٌ ۝ وَلَا تَرْكَنُوٓا۟ إِلَى ٱلَّذِينَ ظَلَمُوا۟ فَتَمَسَّكُمُ ٱلنَّارُ وَمَا لَكُم مِّن دُونِ ٱللَّهِ مِنْ أَوْلِيَآءَ ثُمَّ لَا تُنصَرُونَ ۝ وَأَقِمِ ٱلصَّلَوٰةَ طَرَفَىِ ٱلنَّهَارِ وَزُلَفًا مِّنَ ٱلَّيْلِ إِنَّ ٱلْحَسَنَٰتِ يُذْهِبْنَ ٱلسَّيِّـَٔاتِ ذَٰلِكَ ذِكْرَىٰ لِلذَّٰكِرِينَ ۝ وَٱصْبِرْ فَإِنَّ ٱللَّهَ لَا يُضِيعُ أَجْرَ ٱلْمُحْسِنِينَ ۝ (هود)

Be upright as you have been ordered, you and those who repent along with you, and do not transgress. Verily, He is, regarding all that you do, All-Seeing. And do not incline towards those who have oppressed, lest the Hellfire befall you, whilst you would have no protectors beside Allah, and then you would not be aided. And establish the prayer at the two sides of the day, and at times of closeness within the night as well. Certainly, good deeds do away with bad ones. That is a reminder for all those who remember. And be patient, for verily Allah does not lose the reward of those who do good. (11:112-115)

23.2 TAFSEER BENEFITS

1) The general context of these Verses
2) The meaning of *istiqaamah* according to the rightly guided Caliphs: A) B) C) D)

E) Ibn Rajab summarizes:

3) The foundation of *istiqaamah* and its branches
(30:20)
(Hadeeth)
(Hadeeth)

4) Allah's praise of the people of *istiqaamah*
(41:30)
(46:13-14)

5) Is it possible to maintain complete *istiqaamah* always?
(41:6)
(Hadeeth)

6) "And those who repent along with you..."
(24:31)
(66:8)
(Hadeeth)

7) The meaning of transgression
Ibn al-Qayyim:
As-Sa'dee:
(79:37-41)

8) "He is, regarding all that you do, All-Seeing"

9) Not even inclining towards the oppressors

10) A severely stern warning issue to the Prophet (17:73-75)
11) "You would have no protectors beside Allah..."
12) "And then you would not be aided..."
13) An important deduction about the severity of oppression
14) Ibn 'Abbaas' keen observation (Hadeeth)
15) What are the prayers at the two sides of the day & at night?
16) Good deeds do away with bad ones (Hadeeth)
17) The incident about which 11:114 was revealed (Hadeeth)
18) Which bad deeds are wiped away by good deeds? (4:31) (Hadeeth)
19) "**THAT** [?] is a reminder..."
20) "For all those who remember..."
21) An order to be patient and steadfast
22) "Allah does not lose the reward of those who do good..."

23.3 FATWA: Shaykh 'Abdul-'Azeez ibn Baaz (may Allah have Mercy on him) was asked the following question. Listen and summarize his answer in the box below.

Question: Since the days of Ramadhaan can be made up all year, and the time for six days of Shawwaal is limited, can a person fast the days of Shawwaal before making up the missed days of Ramadhaan?

Shaykh Ibn Baaz replied:

24.1 HADEETH STUDY

عَنْ أَبِي ذَرٍّ ــ رَضِيَ اللهُ عَنْهُ ــ قَالَ: قَالَ لِي رَسُولُ اللهِ ــ صَلَّى اللهُ عَلَيْهِ وَسَلَّمَ ــ :

«اتَّقِ اللهَ حَيْثُمَا كُنْتَ، وَأَتْبِعِ السَّيِّئَةَ الْحَسَنَةَ تَمْحُهَا، وَخَالِقِ النَّاسَ بِخُلُقٍ

حَسَنٍ.» (أَخْرَجَهُ التِّرْمِذِيُّ، وَقَالَ: حَسَنٌ صَحِيحٌ)

On the authority of Aboo Tharr (may Allah be pleased with him): The Messenger of Allah (may Allah raise his rank and grant him peace) said to me: **"Fear Allah wherever you are, follow up a bad deed with a good one and it will wipe it out, and behave well with the people."** (At-Tirmithee)

24.2 BENEFITS OF THE HADEETH

1) Aboo Tharr
2) At-Tirmithee
3) This is hadeeth #_____ of an-Nawawi's famous "40 Hadeeth"
4) Other versions of this hadeeth
5) The lofty status of this hadeeth
6) The meaning of *taqwa* (4:131)

7) Hypocrites hate to hear the reminder: "Fear Allah"

(2:206)

(Hadeeth)

(33:1)

8) *Taqwa* is practiced wherever we are

(31:16)

9) The realistic applicability of the Islamic Legislation

10) With our one single act of repentance, what does Allah do?

A)

B)

C)

D)

E)

F)

G)

11) The importance of upright moral character

(Hadeeth)

(Athar)

12) The definition of upright moral character

A)   B)   C)

13) Recommended resources on the topic of manners:

24.3 FROM YOUR MEMORY: From this lesson; there were seven things mentioned that Allah does when His worshipper repents. List them below from your memory, and then go back to point #10, check your answers, and fill in anything you forgot.

	ALLAH'S ACTIONS RELATIVE TO HIS WORSHIPPER'S REPENTANCE
1	
2	
3	
4	
5	
6	
7	

24.4 FATWA: Shaykh 'Abdul-'Azeez ibn Baaz (may Allah have Mercy on him) was asked the following question. Listen and summarize his answer in the box below.

Question: Some people say there must be a break between the days made up from Ramadhaan and the six days of Shawwaal? Is this correct?

Shaykh Ibn Baaz replied:

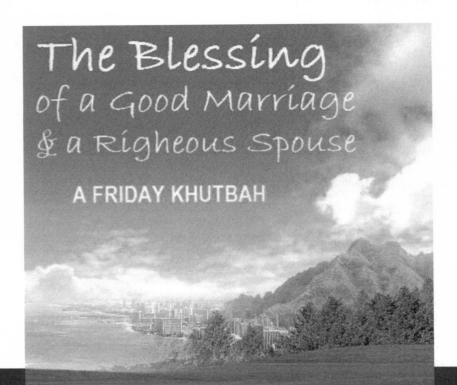

The Blessing
of a Good Marriage
& a Righeous Spouse

A FRIDAY KHUTBAH

ABOO 'ABDIL-FATTAAH SALAAH BROOKS

Recommended recordings from our Spreaker channel

www.Spreaker.com/radio1mm

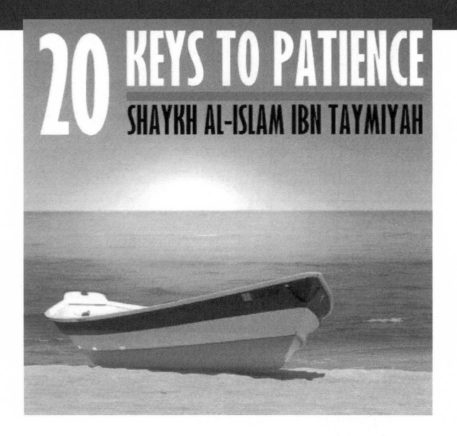

20 KEYS TO PATIENCE
SHAYKH AL-ISLAM IBN TAYMIYAH

25.1 QURANIC PASSAGE & TRANSLATION

أَلَمْ تَرَ كَيْفَ ضَرَبَ ٱللَّهُ مَثَلًا كَلِمَةً طَيِّبَةً كَشَجَرَةٍ طَيِّبَةٍ أَصْلُهَا ثَابِتٌ وَفَرْعُهَا فِى ٱلسَّمَآءِ ۝ تُؤْتِىٓ أُكُلَهَا كُلَّ حِينٍ بِإِذْنِ رَبِّهَا ۗ وَيَضْرِبُ ٱللَّهُ ٱلْأَمْثَالَ لِلنَّاسِ لَعَلَّهُمْ يَتَذَكَّرُونَ ۝ وَمَثَلُ كَلِمَةٍ خَبِيثَةٍ كَشَجَرَةٍ خَبِيثَةٍ ٱجْتُثَّتْ مِن فَوْقِ ٱلْأَرْضِ مَا لَهَا مِن قَرَارٍ ۝ يُثَبِّتُ ٱللَّهُ ٱلَّذِينَ ءَامَنُوا۟ بِٱلْقَوْلِ ٱلثَّابِتِ فِى ٱلْحَيَوٰةِ ٱلدُّنْيَا وَفِى ٱلْأَخِرَةِ ۖ وَيُضِلُّ ٱللَّهُ ٱلظَّٰلِمِينَ ۚ وَيَفْعَلُ ٱللَّهُ مَا يَشَآءُ ۝ (إبراهيم)

Have you not seen how Allah strikes the parable of a good word being similar to a good tree? Its trunk is firm; its branches in the sky. It bears its fruit every so often, by the Permission of its Lord. Allah does strike parables for people, in order for them to reflect. And the likeness of a filthy word is like that of a rotten tree. Uprooted, laying upon the ground, it has no stability to remain. Allah grants stability to those who believe by way of the firm statement, in this life and in the Hereafter. And Allah sends the oppressors astray. Allah does whatever He wills. (14:24-27)

25.2 TAFSEER BENEFITS

1) Who is being addressed: "Have you not seen…?"
2) Similes and metaphors in the Quran and *Sunnah* (2:26) (Hadeeth)

3) The wisdom behind Quranic similes

  A) Ibn al-Qayyim:

  B) As-Sa'dee:

4) The four pillars of a simile

  A)   B)   C)   D)

5) An analysis of the simile involving a good word

  A)   B)   C)   D)

  The overall lesson:

6) The importance of properly understanding Quranic or Prophetic similes

  (Hadeeth)

  What is being compared to what?

  A terrible misunderstanding:

7) How the *Salaf* felt when they could not understand a Quranic simile

  (29:43)

  (Athar)

  (Athar)

8) An analysis of the simile involving a filthy word

  A)   B)   C)   D)

  The overall lesson:

9) Reflecting: Why did Allah create such trees?   C)

  A)   D)

  B)   E)

10) The stability of believers in this life

11) The stability of believers in the Hereafter

12) An amazing benefit from the simile of a good word
13) Can Allah be compared to His Creation? Comparatively: (16:74) (42:11) Superlatively: (16:60) (Hadeeth)
14) The usage of similes to mislead people (25:8-9)
15) Good words come from good people (24:26)

Left: A "Hanthal" (Colocynth) fruit native to the Middle East and Asia.
Below: A vehicle is totally destroyed after colliding with a palm tree.

25.3 ACTIVITY: In the tables below, identify the four essential elements of similes and the overall lessons learned from the following Quranic parables. On your own, find another simile in the Quran for the fourth and final analysis.

A) SIMILE: A GOOD WORD (14:24-25)		
A good word Is being compared to: *A good tree*	Device: *Mathalu, Kaaf (the likeness, is like)*	Intended angle(s) of comparison: *The strength of the foundation* *The ongoing fruits/benefit*
Overall lesson: *The testimony of faith provides long-term stability and benefit.*		

B) SIMILE: A FILTHY WORD (14:26)		
_____ Is being compared to: _____	Device:	Intended angle(s) of comparison:
Overall lesson:		

C) SIMILE: THE DEEDS OF THE DISBELIEVERS (14:18)		
_____ are being compared to _____	Device:	Intended angle(s) of comparison:
Overall lesson:		

D) SIMILE:		
_____ Is being compared to: _____	Device:	Intended angle(s) of comparison:
Overall lesson:		

25.4 FATWA: Shaykh 'Abdul-'Azeez ibn Baaz (may Allah have Mercy on him) was asked the following question. Listen and summarize his answer in the box below.

Question: Is it allowed to make I'tikaaf in any masjid or only in the three great masjids?

Shaykh Ibn Baaz replied:

26.1 HADEETH STUDY

عَنِ ابْنِ مَسْعُودٍ ـ رَضِيَ اللهُ عَنْهُ ـ ، قَالَ: قَالَ رَسُولُ اللهِ ـ صَلَّى اللهُ عَلَيْهِ وَسَلَّمَ ـ :

«لَقِيتُ إِبْرَاهِيمَ لَيْلَةَ أُسْرِيَ بِي، فَقَالَ: يَا مُحَمَّدُ! أَقْرِئْ أُمَّتَكَ مِنِّي السَّلَامَ، وَأَخْبِرْهُمْ أَنَّ الجَنَّةَ طَيِّبَةُ التُّرْبَةِ، عَذْبَةُ الْمَاءِ، وَأَنَّهَا قِيعَانٌ، وَأَنَّ غِرَاسَهَا: سُبْحَانَ اللهِ، وَالْحَمْدُ لِلَّهِ، وَلَا إِلَهَ إِلَّا اللهُ، وَاللهُ أَكْبَرُ.» (أَخْرَجَهُ التِّرْمِذِيُّ، وَقَالَ: حَسَنٌ غَرِيبٌ)

On the authority of Ibn Mas'ood (may Allah be pleased with him): The Messenger of Allah (may Allah raise his rank and grant him peace) said: "I met **Ibraaheem on the night I was taken on a journey, and he said: 'O Muhammad! Convey the** *salaams* **from me to your** *Ummah***, and tell them that Paradise has pure, fertile ground and sweet water, and that it is open and uncultivated. Its seeds are: Exalted is Allah, all praise is due to Allah, there is no one worthy of worship other than Allah, and Allah is the Greatest.'"** (At-Tirmithee)

26.2 BENEFITS OF THE HADEETH

1) Ibn Mas'ood
2) At-Tirmithee
3) The authenticity of the hadeeth
4) Ibraaheem   (2:127-132)
5) The Night Journey   (17:1)
6) The greeting of Ibraaheem

7) The fertile ground of Paradise described
8) The water of Paradise described
9) The meaning of "qee'aan"
10) Seeds planted in Paradise
11) "Subhaan Allaah"
12) "Al-hamdu lillaah"
13) "Laa ilaaha ill Allaah"
14) "Allaahu akbar"

15) Virtues of these four phrases
 	
   (Hadeeth)
 	
   (Hadeeth)

16) Connecting this hadeeth to Quran (14:24-27)
17) Connecting this hadeeth to Quran (18:46)

26.3 FATWA: Shaykh 'Abdul-'Azeez ibn Baaz (may Allah have Mercy on him) was asked the following question. Listen and summarize his answer in the box below.

Question: Is it from the Sunnah to take time off from work to focus solely on worship in the month of Ramadhaan?

Shaykh Ibn Baaz replied:

THE FUTILITY OF FALSE OBJECTS OF WORSHIP

27.1 QURANIC PASSAGE & TRANSLATION

وَالَّذِينَ يَدْعُونَ مِن دُونِ اللَّهِ لَا يَخْلُقُونَ شَيْئًا وَهُمْ يُخْلَقُونَ ﴿٢٠﴾ أَمْوَاتٌ غَيْرُ أَحْيَاءٍ ۖ وَمَا يَشْعُرُونَ أَيَّانَ يُبْعَثُونَ ﴿٢١﴾ إِلَٰهُكُمْ إِلَٰهٌ وَاحِدٌ ۚ فَالَّذِينَ لَا يُؤْمِنُونَ بِالْآخِرَةِ قُلُوبُهُم مُّنكِرَةٌ وَهُم مُّسْتَكْبِرُونَ ﴿٢٢﴾ لَا جَرَمَ أَنَّ اللَّهَ يَعْلَمُ مَا يُسِرُّونَ وَمَا يُعْلِنُونَ ۚ إِنَّهُ لَا يُحِبُّ الْمُسْتَكْبِرِينَ ﴿٢٣﴾ (النحل)

Those whom they call upon besides Allah do not create anything, while they themselves are created. Dead things, not even alive, and they do not even sense when they will be resurrected. Your rightful object of worship is one God. Those who do not believe in the Hereafter have hearts in denial, and they are arrogant. In reality, Allah knows all that they do secretly and openly. Verily, He does not love the arrogant. (16:20-23)

27.2 TAFSEER BENEFITS

1) A logical appeal	
2) Quranic method of disqualifying false objects of worship	

3) Attributes of false objects of worship:	Attributes they DO NOT have:
A)	D)
B)	E)
C)	F)

4) "They do not even sense when they will be resurrected..."   A)   B)
5) "Dead things, not even alive..."
6) "Your rightful object of worship is one God..."
7) Summarizing disbelief as rejection of a single pillar of faith   (17:10)   (17:45)   (27:4)   (39:45)   (53:27)
8) Hearts in denial   (39:45)
9) The phrase: *"Laa jarama"*
10) "Allah knows all that they do secretly and openly..."
11) The severe offense of arrogance   (40:60)   (Hadeeth)
12) How central supplication is as an act of worship   (40:60)   (Hadeeth)   (Hadeeth)

13) Sufi misguidance   (False narration)
14) An important reminder about manners   (6:108)   *Review: Lesson #19 (Hadeeth #23) of the course: 130 Hadeeth on Manners*

27.3 FATWA: Shaykh 'Abdul-'Azeez ibn Baaz (may Allah have Mercy on him) was asked the following question. Listen and summarize his answer in the box below.

Question: Do I have to discharge Zakaat al-Fitr on behalf of my little sister, after the passing of our father?

> **Shaykh Ibn Baaz replied:**

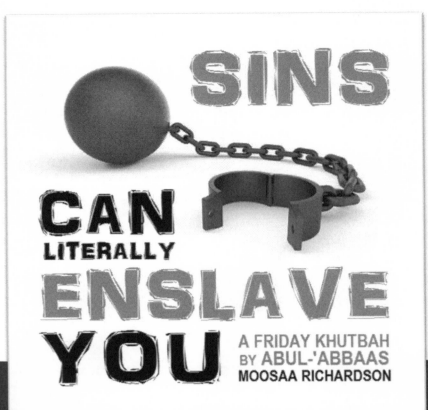

SINS CAN LITERALLY ENSLAVE YOU

A FRIDAY KHUTBAH BY ABUL-'ABBAAS MOOSAA RICHARDSON

Recommended recordings from our Spreaker channel

www.Spreaker.com/radio1mm

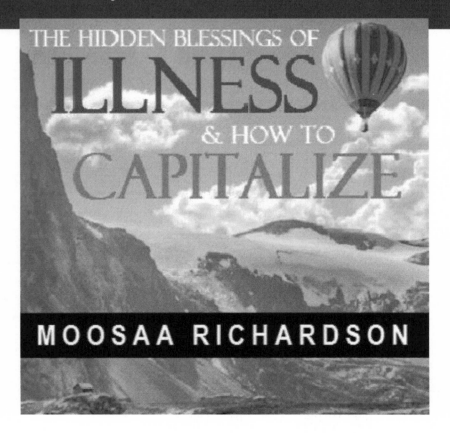

THE HIDDEN BLESSINGS OF ILLNESS & HOW TO CAPITALIZE

MOOSAA RICHARDSON

CLOSING OFF THE PATHWAYS TO POLYTHEISM

28.1 HADEETH & TRANSLATION

عَنْ أَبِي بَشِيرٍ الْأَنْصَارِيِّ ــ رَضِيَ اللهُ عَنْهُ ــ : أَنَّهُ كَانَ مَعَ رَسُولِ اللهِ ــ صَلَّى اللهُ عَلَيْهِ وَسَلَّمَ ــ فِي بَعْضِ أَسْفَارِهِ، قَالَ: فَأَرْسَلَ رَسُولُ اللهِ ــ صَلَّى اللهُ عَلَيْهِ وَسَلَّمَ ــ رَسُولًا، وَالنَّاسُ فِي مَبِيتِهِمْ: «لَا يَبْقَيَنَّ فِي رَقَبَةِ بَعِيرٍ قِلَادَةٌ مِنْ وَتَرٍ، أَوْ قِلَادَةٌ، إِلَّا قُطِعَتْ.» (مُتَّفَقٌ عَلَيْهِ)

On the authority of Aboo Basheer al-Ansaaree (may Allah be pleased with him): He was with the Messenger of Allah (May Allah raise his rank and grant him peace) on one of his journeys. The Messenger of Allah (may Allah raise his rank and grant him peace) dispatched a messenger to the people while they were at their tents, [to proclaim]: **"There must not remain around the neck of any camel any bowstring, or any string, except that it is to be cut off."** (Agreed upon)

28.2 BENEFITS OF THE HADEETH

1) Aboo Basheer
2) Agreed upon
3) The overall meaning of the hadeeth
4) Al-Bukhaaree's chapter title

5) A wording added by Muslim:

6) Three understandings offered by the scholars:

A)

B)

C)

7) What is not included in the meaning of the hadeeth

8) Talismans hung to ward off evil

9) Major *shirk* (polytheism) vs. lesser *shirk*

10) Forbidding evil

(Hadeeth)

11) Focusing on creed and its proper application

12) Teaching people during journeys

13) What about "Quranic amulets"?

14) A modern application: Around the necks of camels

15) A clarification of misunderstandings on the topic:

28.3 FATWA: Shaykh 'Abdul-'Azeez ibn Baaz (may Allah have Mercy on him) was asked the following question. Listen and summarize his answer in the box below.

Question: In what city should I discharge my Zakaat al-Fitr if I travel near the end of Ramadhaan?

Shaykh Ibn Baaz replied:

29.1 QURANIC PASSAGE & TRANSLATION

﴿ وَكُلَّ إِنسَانٍ أَلْزَمْنَاهُ طَائِرَهُ فِى عُنُقِهِ وَنُخْرِجُ لَهُ يَوْمَ الْقِيَامَةِ كِتَابًا يَلْقَاهُ مَنشُورًا ﴿١٣﴾ اقْرَأْ كِتَابَكَ كَفَى بِنَفْسِكَ الْيَوْمَ عَلَيْكَ حَسِيبًا ﴿١٤﴾ مَّنِ اهْتَدَى فَإِنَّمَا يَهْتَدِى لِنَفْسِهِ وَمَن ضَلَّ فَإِنَّمَا يَضِلُّ عَلَيْهَا وَلَا تَزِرُ وَازِرَةٌ وِزْرَ أُخْرَى وَمَا كُنَّا مُعَذِّبِينَ حَتَّى نَبْعَثَ رَسُولًا ﴿١٥﴾ ﴾ (الإسراء)

For each person, We have fastened his deeds upon his own neck, and then We shall bring it forth for him on the Day of Judgment, as a book which he encounters, spread open. "Read your book; it is sufficient on this Day as an account kept against you." Whoever is guided is only guided for his own self, and whoever strays only strays against his own self. No one shall bear the burdens of another person, and We would never punish [anyone] without first sending a Messenger. (17:13-15)

29.2 TAFSEER BENEFITS

1. What is a *"taa'ir"*?	
2. What is the significance of that being fastened to one's "neck" specifically?	
3. Linguistic devices emphasizing singularity	F)
A)	G)
B)	H)
C)	I)
D)	J)
E)	K)

4) Shunning false excuses and cop-outs *"I've just been so busy with work..."*
5) Everything is written [Ibn 'Uthaymeen] (81:10) (50:18) (Hadeeth) (Hadeeth)
6) Noble scribes writing everything [Ibn 'Uthaymeen] (82:10-12) Perfect justice: (24:24) (41:21)
7) Uprightness and wickedness is only for or against you yourself
8) Focus on yourself heavily; the misguidance of others is no excuse. (5:105) *Review: Lesson 20 (of this book).*
9) "No one shall bear the burdens of another person" (Hadeeth) Response A: Response B:
10) "We would never punish anyone without first sending a Messenger"
11) Applying this to non-Muslim children who die young

12) The narration of the *"imtihaan"* (test)

Four people: A) _____ B) _____ C) _____ D) _____

Rationale vs. obedience

29.3 REMINDER: Be sure that you have either distributed your *Zakaat al-Fitr* by now, or you have prepared it for distribution. Offer your assistance to those who may need help in doing so.

WHAT: *Zakaat al-Fitr* is distributed as three liters (about 6.6 pounds/3 kilograms to be safe) of dry staple foods (like wheat, flour, barley, rice, etc.).

WHO PAYS IT: The head of each household, on behalf of all those under his care.

HOW MUCH: One amount (as described in "WHAT" above) for each person under your care, including yourself. *Example:* A man with a wife and four children (six people) distributes 18 liters (6x3) of food (or 18 kilograms, or 39.6 pounds).

TO WHOM: Poor Muslims of your land.

WHEN: Before the *'Eed al-Fitr* Prayer (or a day or two before that).

WHY: A compensation for deficiencies in one's fast, taking care of the needy

Review: Last year's Ramadhaan Lessons: Lesson 21 about Zakaat al-Fitr, if needed.

29.4 FATWA: Shaykh 'Abdul-'Azeez ibn Baaz (may Allah have Mercy on him) was asked the following question. Listen and summarize his answer in the box below.

Question: Can I discharge my Zakaat al-Fitr as money, instead of food?

Shaykh Ibn Baaz replied:

29.5 ACTIVITY: Read the article entitled: *15 Reasons to Give out Your Own Zakaat al-Fitr Yourself (Part One)*, and summarize the first eight reasons in the table below:

	REASONS TO GIVE OUT OUR *ZAKAAT AL-FITR* OURSELVES
1	Building bridges with poor people who have virtue
2	
3	
4	
5	
6	
7	
8	

1 – We will build bridges with poor people and get to know them personally.

Poor people are virtuous. The Messenger (may Allaah raise his rank and grant him peace) said, what means, **"I saw Paradise and most of its people were the poor (of this life)."** [2]

And another authentic hadeeth means, **"The impoverished shall enter Paradise before the rich by 500 years."** [3]

So by seeking them out and giving them your *Zakaat al-Fitr*, you may gain the companionship of the righteous, even for a short time. This benefit is lost when giving through a third party.

Instead of saying, *"But I don't know any poor families, so how could I give out my zakaat al-Fitr personally...?"*

30.1 HADEETH & TRANSLATION

عَنِ ابْنِ عُمَرَ ــ رَضِيَ اللهُ عَنْهُمَا ــ ، قَالَ: قَلَّمَا كَانَ رَسُولُ اللهِ ــ صَلَّى اللهُ عَلَيْهِ وَسَلَّمَ ــ يَقُومُ مِنْ مَجْلِسٍ حَتَّى يَدْعُوَ بِهَؤُلَاءِ الدَّعَوَاتِ لِأَصْحَابِهِ: «اللّهُمَّ اقْسِمْ لَنَا مِنْ خَشْيَتِكَ مَا يَـــحُولُ بَيْنَنَا وَبَيْنَ مَعَاصِيكَ، وَمِنْ طَاعَتِكَ مَا تُبَلِّغُنَا بِهِ جَنَّتَكَ، وَمِنَ الْيَقِينِ مَا تُهَوِّنُ بِهِ عَلَيْنَا مُصِيبَاتِ الدُّنْيَا، وَمَتِّعْنَا بِأَسْـــمَاعِنَا وَأَبْصَارِنَا وَقُوَّتِنَا مَا أَحْيَيْتَنَا، وَاجْعَلْهُ الْوَارِثَ مِنَّا، وَاجْعَلْ ثَأْرَنَا عَلَى مَنْ ظَلَمَنَا، وَانْصُرْنَا عَلَى مَنْ عَادَانَا، وَلَا تَجْعَلْ مُصِيبَتَنَا فِي دِينِنَا، وَلَا تَجْعَلِ الدُّنْيَا أَكْبَرَ هَمِّنَا وَلَا مَبْلَغَ عِلْمِنَا، وَلَا تُسَلِّطْ عَلَيْنَا مَنْ لَا يَرْحَمُنَا.» (أَخْرَجَهُ التِّرْمِذِيُّ)

Ibn 'Umar (may Allah be pleased with him) said: Rarely would the Messenger of Allah (may Allah raise his rank and grant him peace) get up from any gathering without supplicating with the following prayers for his Companions: "**O Allah! Grant us a share of fear of You, enough to come between us and disobedience to You. And [grant us] of Your obedience what would cause us to reach your Paradise. And [grant us] of certainty what would make the calamities of this life easier upon us. Allow us to enjoy our hearing, eyesight, and physical strength so long as you keep us alive, and make that what is inherited from us. Enact our revenge upon those who oppress us, and give us victory over those who have animosity for us. Do not make our trials religious ones, and do not make worldly matters the greatest of our concerns, nor the extent of our knowledge. And do not give reign over us to those who would not have mercy on us.**" (At-Tirmithee)

30.2 BENEFITS OF THE HADEETH

1) Ibn 'Umar
2) At-Tirmithee
3) Rarely would he get up without supplicating with this
4) The meaning of *"khashyah"* (35:28) What else is necessarily included in this request?
5) The fruit of this *"khashyah"* (67:12) Ibn 'Uthaymeen said:
6) The goal of obedience to Allah (4:13) (33:71) (4:69-70)
7) Combining between fear and obedience (24:52)
8) The meaning of *"yaqeen"* The highest kind of faith (102:5-6) What else is necessarily included in this request?
9) The trials of this life (Hadeeth) (2:155) (Hadeeth) (Hadeeth)

10) Requesting the preservation of our faculties (Hadeeth) Abut-Tayyib at-Tabaree
11) "Make that what is inherited from us..."
12) The ruling on supplicating against oppressors (Hadeeth)
13) Our request for retribution (Hadeeth) (11:102)
14) Requesting victory and aid (2:214) (3:160) (8:10) (47:7)
15) "Do not make our trials religious ones..."
16) "Do not make worldly matters our greatest concern..."
17) Refuge sought from merciless authorities What else is necessarily included in this request?
18) The pathway to honor and distinction (24:55) (Hadeeth)

30.3 ACTIVITY: From the supplication we just studied, summarize the ten matters which we are asking for directly, noting what that also includes indirectly in the table below.

#	Directly	Indirectly
1	Sincere, effective khashyah	Not hypocritical khashyah
2	Sincere obedience	
3		
4		
5		
6		
7		
8		
9		
10		

30.4 FATWA: Shaykh 'Abdul-'Azeez ibn Baaz (may Allah have Mercy on him) was asked the following question. Listen and summarize his answer in the box below.

Question: Are there Sunnah prayers to be offered before the Eed Prayer?

Shaykh Ibn Baaz replied:

AL-HAMDU LILLAAH

This completes our study of these thirty passages from the Quran and Sunnah, and all praise is due to Allah, the only One who facilitates success.

رَّبَّنَآ إِنَّنَا سَمِعْنَا مُنَادِيًا يُنَادِي لِلْإِيمَـٰنِ أَنْ ءَامِنُوا۟ بِرَبِّكُمْ فَـَٔامَنَّا

رَبَّنَا فَٱغْفِرْ لَنَا ذُنُوبَنَا وَكَفِّرْ عَنَّا سَيِّـَٔاتِنَا

وَتَوَفَّنَا مَعَ ٱلْأَبْرَارِ

آل عمران

١٩٣

Our Lord! We have heard a caller calling to eemaan,
saying: 'Believe in your Lord!' So we have believed.

Our Lord! Forgive us for our sins,
and expiate from us our bad deeds.

And take our souls
along with the
righteous.

[3:193]

FATWAS BY SHAYKH IBN BAAZ

FATWA 1: The Number of Witnesses Needed to Begin the Month — 12

FATWA 2: Relying Solely on Calculations & Ignoring Moon Sightings — 15

FATWA 3: Fasting a 31-Day Ramadhaan? — 20

FATWA 4: The Fasting of a Person Who Does Not Pray — 22

FATWA 5: Should We Instruct Young Children to Fast? — 26

FATWA 6: Did Not Make Up Last Ramadhaan's Missed Days — 30

FATWA 7: Someone Who Did Not Start Fasting Until After Puberty — 34

FATWA 8: What if a Woman Comes Off Her Menses Just Before *Fajr*? — 38

FATWA 9: A Traveler Using Comfortable Means of Transportation — 42

FATWA 10: Students Breaking Fast Because of Difficult Final Exams? — 45

FATWA 11: Dental Work and Local Anesthetics During the Fast — 49

FATWA 12: Toothpaste, Ear Drops, Eye Drops, Nose Drops — 53

FATWA 13: Does Vomiting Break the Fast? — 58

FATWA 14: Masturbation During the Days of Ramadhaan — 60

FATWA 15: Nosebleeds, Bloodwork, Donating Blood — 64

FATWA 16: Prayer Schedules That Have a Time for "*Imsaak*" — 66

FATWA 17: Sleeping Past *Suhoor* Time, Missing *Suhoor* — 70

FATWA 18: Traveling By Plane Westward, Day Gets Longer — 74

FATWA 19: Breaking the Fast Because of General Difficulty — 78

FATWA 20: Must Consecutive Missed Days Be Made Up Consecutively? — 81

FATWA 21: Repenting After Years of Neglected Prayers and Fasting — 85

FATWA 22: Making Up the Recommended Days of Shawwaal — 90

FATWA 23: Optional Fasting Before Making Up Missed Days? — 94

FATWA 24: A Required Break Between Making Up Days & Shawwaal? — 97

FATWA 25: *I'tikaaf* in Any Masjid or Only the Main Three? — 103

FATWA 26: Taking Time Off Work to Worship in Ramadhaan — 106

FATWA 27: *Zakaat al-Fitr* for Younger Siblings After the Father's Death — 109

FATWA 28: In Which City Should I Discharge *Zakaat al-Fitr* if I Travel? — 113

FATWA 29: Discharging *Zakaat al-Fitr* as Money Instead of Food — 117

FATWA 30: *Sunnah* Prayers Before the *'Eed* Prayer? — 122

Made in the USA
Middletown, DE
23 April 2019